THE BLACK BOOK *of* SOUL

AF552491

Know everything about Soul &
Reboot yourself for new beginnings

DEEP TRIVEDI

Author of the Bestseller 'I am The Mind'

DEEP TRIVEDI The Speaker

Deep Trivedi uses a unique combination of psycho-spiritual content, voice, language and expression, which effectuates an instantaneous transformation in his viewers and listeners. Innumerable lives have been transformed just by listening to him. This is the reason why he is known as a pioneer in spiritual psychodynamics.

Deep Trivedi sheds light on every subject related to life. His interactive workshops have brought about a revolutionary transformation in people's lives by addressing their day-to-day concerns. There is no aspect of human life that has been left untouched by him. He has spoken on Bhagavad Gita, Tao Te Ching, Ashtavakra Gita, 'Secrets of Nature, Mind, Soul, Time, Destiny', so on and so forth and numerous topics such as:

- **Ego**
- **God**
- **Guilt**
- **Love**
- **Anger**
- **Future**
- **Wealth**
- **Phobias**
- **Religion**
- **Complex**
- **Marriage**
- **Freedom**
- **Partiality**
- **Day-Sleep**
- **DNA-Genes**
- **Path of Life**
- **Personality**
- **Expectation**
- **Acceptance**
- **Hypocrisy**
- **Creativity**
- **Confusion**
- **Good-Bad**
- **Involvement**
- **Concentration**
- **Laws of Nature**
- **Time and Space**
- **Mind and Brain**
- **Self-Confidence**
- **Joy and Happiness**
- **Natural Intelligence**
- **Power of Transformation**

DVDs and Audio CDs of his lectures and workshops on the above topics and many more are available on **www.aatmanestore.com** and other leading e-commerce sites.

DEEP TRIVEDI

DEEP TRIVEDI

Deep Trivedi is a renowned author, speaker and pioneer in spiritual psychodynamics. He writes and conducts lectures as well as workshops with an all-pervasive perspective, guiding individuals towards the achievement of their full potential. To date, he has led thousands of people onto the path of success and happiness through his works.

In his voluminous works, Deep Trivedi has extensively explained Nature, its laws, its behaviour, its psychology and the effect it has on human life. No aspect of life and human psychology has been left untouched by him. He states that lack of psychological knowledge and understanding is the sole reason for all the sorrows and failures that pervade human life.

He has authored bestsellers such as 'I am The Mind', 'I am Krishna' and many more. His bestseller 'I am The Mind' has been published in several national and international languages. He has been awarded the Times Power Men Award 2018 for his immense contribution to society.

His command over the biggest psychologies of life can be gauged by the fact that he holds the record for 'Maximum Lectures on Human Life', 'Maximum Lectures on Psychological

DEEP TRIVEDI

Aspects of Tao Te Ching', 'Maximum Lectures on Ashtavakra Gita' and 'Maximum Lectures on Bhagavad Gita', spanning 168 hours, 28 minutes, 50 seconds in 58 days in different National and International record books. He also holds the record for 'Maximum Number of Quotations on Human Life' (about 12038) on subjects such as Soul, Human Life, Psychology, Laws of Nature, Destiny and many more. He has also been awarded an Honorary Doctorate for his Psychological works on the Bhagavad Gita. His interactive workshops have brought about a revolutionary transformation in people's lives by addressing their day-to-day concerns. These lectures and workshops have been delivered in front of live audiences across India.

He is known for his special ability to touch upon the deepest aspects of life and explain them by using lucid language, leaving no scope for ambiguity. The distinct spiritual-psychological language and expression in his writings, lectures and workshops, begin to have an instant effect on the mind of the reader or listener, which makes Deep Trivedi a pioneer in this field.

To know more about Deep Trivedi, visit www.deeptrivedi.com

Contents

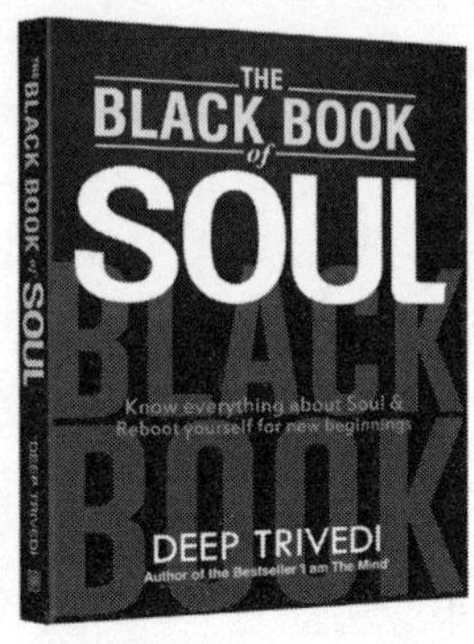

First Edition: 2020
Price: Rs 299/-

Printed in India

Concept, Illustration and Design:

www.aatmaninnovations.com

Publisher: Aatman Innovations Pvt. Ltd.
Place of Publication: Mumbai

ISBN 978-93-84850-78-4

All Rights Reserved.

No part of this publication may be reproduced, stored in a retrieval system or transmitted in any form or by any means, electronic, mechanical, photocopying, recording or otherwise, without the prior written permission of the publisher.

Copyright © Aatman Innovations Pvt. Ltd.

The Secret of All Secrets!

One life, yet queries galore!
This is the paradox of human life.

Ideally, if one is born as a human being, his life must thrive; it must brim with laughter, joy and success. But unfortunately, that is not the case! Why? This 'why' has confounded the entire human race for ages. However, in the present-day age of science and technology, when most of the existential questions have been answered, it is high time that we seek the answer to this question as well. And in order to arrive at the right answer, it is imperative to first decide – whose responsibility it is? For, it is certain that the human being is leading an unsuccessful existence. In that case, the only question that remains to be answered is – Who is responsible for this? Is the human being himself to be blamed? And if the entire blame were to rest with human beings, the very next question would be – Does a human being really enjoy absolute freedom? For, only if a human being is absolutely free can he be held fully responsible. In the second case, if a human being does not enjoy full freedom, then what are the powers that influence human life? By and large, if the answers to these two questions are found, the mystery of human life could be unravelled. Only then, would it be possible for every human being to attain happiness and success.

Well, speaking of freedom, in comparison to the stars, moon, air, water, or for that matter even birds and animals, a human being certainly appears to enjoy greater freedom. But, even then, a question remains to be answered—is a human being completely free or only partially—that is to say, is he bound by certain influences too? In this regard, one must clearly understand that there are several mysterious powers of Nature that influence human life and their influences need to be comprehended thoroughly. This is because, although a human being has freedom, he is bound by the laws of several powers of Nature.

To make it easier for you to comprehend, I shall elucidate this with the help of an example. For this, you shall have to carry out an experiment. First, stand up straight. Then, raise one leg. You may raise your left or right leg. The choice rests with you. Now, try to raise the other one. Got you, didn't I!? This time, you are left with no choice as you had already made one when you raised your first leg. Well, now you need to understand that this is the extent of freedom a human enjoys. You can draw an analogy between this situation and the extent of freedom a human enjoys. You are free to choose whether you want to raise the left leg or the right, but once the choice is made, you are bound by the various mysterious laws of Nature to bear the consequences for the same.

At this stage, it is imperative to comprehend that all secret forces of Nature are paradoxical. If you comprehend this in the context of human freedom, you would realise that while, on the one hand, a human enjoys total freedom, on the other, he is bound by the consequences of the choices he makes. In other words, he is free to take the step of his choice, but once the step is taken, he is bound to bear the consequences for the same. Hence, it is incorrect to state that a human being is totally free, but at the same time, it is also erroneous to state that he is not free. The truth lies in between these two statements. This very paradox exists in all secret forces of Nature. But as the common man does not possess the knowledge of the paradoxicality that exists in these secret forces of Nature, he is delusional with regards to life. Some espouse atheism in the name of freedom, while others, in view of human dependence or lack of freedom, advocate religious ritualism. But, as both these views are fallacious, neither of them is able to transform human life or help one have a better understanding of it.

Well, so far, we have grasped the greatest paradox concerning human life that a human being is free as well as bound. However, not everyone must have necessarily understood this at the first instance; hence, let me draw yet another analogy between the above-mentioned paradox and a restaurant. Suppose you were to visit a Chinese restaurant for a meal; perhaps of your own free will or under someone's influence or pressure. Needless to say, if you wish to follow your own will, then you have the freedom not to be compelled by anyone. Whether you go there out of your own will or someone else's, in any case, once you are at the restaurant, you are free to order the food of your choice. However, this freedom binds you with a limitation. You can only order a dish that is available at the restaurant.

The same analogy is applicable to life too. You are free to choose a restaurant, but once chosen, you are bound to select from the varieties available there. Now returning to the earlier point of making a choice, what one might prefer, would of course, depend on several factors such as, one's background, place of birth, the culture, the environment and the circumstances one has been raised in. And in this case too, the human mind and the secret forces of Nature both collectively become the decisive factors. In other words, there is a constant interplay of human freedom and the limitations that one is bound by and it is this very interplay that determines everything in human life.

Simply put, without comprehending the intricacies of this interplay, life cannot be changed for the better. To understand this interplay, one shall have to minutely grasp the functioning of the human mind and the secret forces of Nature, one by one. As soon as this understanding is achieved, we shall find the answers to all questions related to human life. It is with the aim of revealing this secret behind all secrets that I am penning several books on the powers that influence human life such as human mind, human psychology, composition of the mind and its functioning, and on the various powers of Nature that influence a human being like Time, *Karma* (action) and its fruit, birth and rebirth, automation, Laws of Nature and so on and so forth. These books shall certainly help everyone grasp where and why they are trapped in life and also help them comprehend how to break free of this trap. And once these two points are apprehended, it would not take long for a human being to manoeuvre life in the right direction and make it worthwhile.

Importantly, I would like to elucidate here that whether it is the human mind or the secret forces of Nature, both are governed by laws. Hence, it is possible to not only grasp, but also analyse both of them; most importantly, because life cannot be oriented towards the right direction without aligning the human mind with the secret forces of Nature. However, I would also like to clarify that it is not necessary to read or comprehend all this to attune your mind with the secret forces of Nature. There exists a mechanism in Nature for every human being to elevate his mind and immediately lead a life in sync with Nature's secret forces. Whether this takes place wittingly or unwittingly, rest assured that only he, who is living in sync with Nature, can lead a great life. If one harks back to world history, no great person's life has been an exception to this truth. All eminent personalities have achieved legendary greatness only by being in sync with Nature. In other words, all prominent people have achieved greatness by elevating their minds to supreme heights. They were not necessarily aware of the secrets of mind, life or Nature. I am stating this fact, because knowledge of these secret forces is not as significant as being in tune with these secret forces.

In brief, a human being is absolutely free to lead his life as per his wishes. But with every step that he takes, he becomes bound to the consequences by virtue of the various powers of Nature that function according to set laws. And suffering the consequences of his actions is at the root of all human failures. If a human being wants to save himself from adverse consequences, then there is only one way—to flow in sync with the powers of Nature. And one can flow with these powers of Nature either by grasping the secrets of these powers or by aligning oneself with them. In either case, it is certain that without seamlessly flowing in sync with these powers, one cannot attain legendary greatness. In other words, a human being is certainly free, but with the help of this freedom alone, he cannot carve a great life for himself. In order to achieve historic greatness, he will have to align his freedom with the powers of Nature. Hence, if a person presumes that he can elevate himself to greatness solely on the basis of his own decisions and knowledge, then to be honest, he is living in a fool's paradise.

This point can best be elucidated with the analogy of an airplane. Life is like an airplane. The pilot has to take it to a certain height, and then, he just has to put the airplane on 'auto-pilot' mode and sit back to enjoy the flight. Of course, he still has to remain ever vigilant. The same is the case with human life. A human being simply has to elevate his mind to a certain height. As soon as the mind is elevated, the secret powers of Nature take charge of his life. Once they take charge, these powers steer his life towards its ultimate goal. Thereupon, that human being has to do nothing in life, except for remaining aware and alert. The ancient wise people called this virtue of alertness—'living life with total awareness'.

In a nutshell, the most important lessons to progress and carve a great life are those that can catapult the human mind to greater heights. Hence, while understanding the secret powers of Nature, focus on how to elevate the mind by way of your actions, and then, once attuned with the secret powers of Nature, surrender everything to them and just focus on how to enjoy the journey of life. However, while enjoying this journey, you must also maintain awareness and alertness at all times. Thereafter, you will never be besieged by predicaments and confusions whatsoever.

Hence, I am not only hopeful, but also sure that by reading my books based on various secret forces of Nature, all queries related to human life will be put to rest once and for all. And it is with this conviction that I shall be presenting a series of these books for you to peruse at regular intervals.

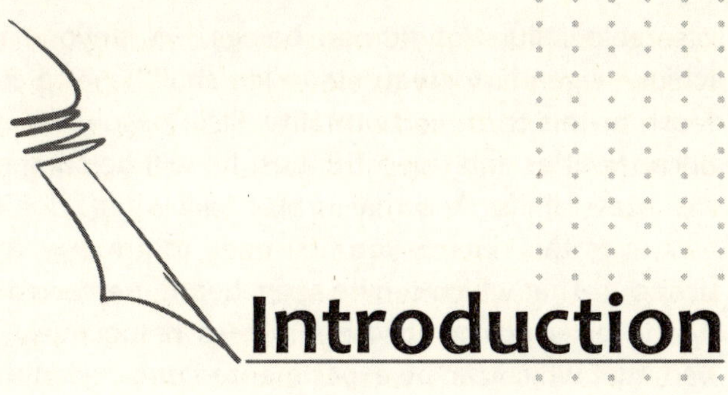

Introduction

In order to understand and delve deep into any secret of Nature, we must be aware of both the visible and invisible worlds that are functioning in tandem with each other. It is also imperative to comprehend that the cause of all that unfolds in the 'visible' lies in the 'invisible'. In other words, although the play of life unfolds in the visible world, its reins lie with the 'invisible'. However, oblivious to this truth, a human being leads his entire life, focussing on the 'visible' alone. He desires to attain everything in the visible world, and to that effect, he continues to make incessant efforts in the visible world alone. But this is where he falters. For, what can be gained by making efforts in a realm that has no power? What can be gained by making efforts for 'that which is inconsequential'?

In short, a human being applies his energy in the wrong direction in the fallacious hope of bettering his life. This is the reason why, in spite of all his efforts, he fails to carve a great life for himself. Hence, everyone must grasp that only if one uses one's energy in comprehending and transforming the 'invisible' instead of the 'visible', one would be able to build a great life for oneself. Honestly speaking, 'not doing so' is actually the root cause of such miserable failure of human beings. So, anyone who wishes to achieve legendary greatness in life shall have to comprehend the depth of this truth in its totality. Else, despite being blessed with all capabilities and opportunities, he will be compelled to lead an unsuccessful life. And that is precisely what I don't want to see...

In this regard, you first need to grasp what the 'visible' is all about. That which can be seen, heard, perceived or experienced by the eyes, ears and other senses respectively is the 'visible'. Also, that which can be experimented upon scientifically, or can be tested and proven in a science laboratory is the 'visible'. And this 'visible' is but one aspect of life. However, the actual human life stems from the 'invisible', it is based in the 'invisible' and is, in fact, influenced by the 'invisible'. And this fact should be etched in your mind forever!

Now, the next question arises as to what is the 'invisible'. The human mind and all human emotions such as happiness, sorrow, worry, joy, etc. constitute the 'invisible'. In fact, the ebb and flow of these emotions constitute the actual human life. This human life, constituted by one's invisible emotions, is influenced by various invisible secret powers such as Time and automation. In other words, human life actually keeps revolving around these two 'invisibles', and the outcomes of human life are thus determined by these two. Once this is grasped, everything else will become easy for you to comprehend. As once one realises the power of the invisible emotions and the authority of the 'invisible secret powers of Nature', one can at least make earnest efforts to further understand them in depth.

It is not that a human being is completely clueless about these invisible powers! Since time immemorial, various discussions have been held on them, and numerous concepts—from 'Destiny' to 'God'—are the results of the discussions on these 'invisibles'. However, at this stage, we will not delve into how right or wrong these discussions are. At present, we need to focus upon the fact that the actual reins of life lie with the invisible. Many believe this and many others have experienced this, and down through the ages, many wise savants have pointed in this direction too. In other words, we are not completely unaware of the invisible powers. However, it has been a general belief that the invisible influences of the mind and the invisible secret forces of Nature can neither be grasped in depth nor can their existence be proved. At the most, one can have faith in them. And I strongly object to this fallacious notion. Does it bode well to hold this view, especially in the present age when science rules the roost!? For, the question arises, how can a human being have faith in something that cannot be proved? Also, the question arises as to why should a human being repose faith in it in the first place? Such superficial faith not only encourages unscrupulous trade in religion, but also fortifies the illusion in human minds. Hence, this issue cannot be dealt with by having superficial faith. In fact, secrets have remained secrets till now only due to emphasis being laid upon having faith alone.

Well, agreed that these secret forces are invisible and profound! Yet, these secret forces belong to this very world! Moreover, the secrets of the mind and Nature are not random in nature; they all are bound by laws. Hence, it is my firm belief that they can always be scientifically analysed, and can also be proved. And only once their existence is proved, will the human being of the present scientific age be able to benefit from these secret powers. Otherwise, we would simply be indulging in idle talk; and baseless talks have only cost humans dearly.

In view of these facts and in order to bring about a revolutionary transformation in human life, I have decided to not only speak of and write about these invisible powers with a scientific approach but also prove their existence at the right junctures. This is because, psychologically, there does not exist an invisible power in Nature that cannot be fathomed. At the same time, there is no height of the mind that an aware human being cannot experience within. And anything that can be explained and experienced can also be proven. This is, indeed, a very profound and unique attempt, and for the upliftment of humanity, it is extremely important. I am sure, I would be able to fulfil this duty diligently and meticulously. Once this task is accomplished, human beings will not have to rely upon mere faith, empty talks or absurd religious assurances. Just as anything proved by Science is never debated, discussions with regards to apprehensions on the functioning of the secret powers of Nature must also cease. If Science stakes claims of the ability to fly in the air, today, we can witness airplanes flying around. Then where does it leave the scope for any faith, doubt or debate?

Hence, I wish to explain all the invisible powers and their laws with the same scientific approach. I also wish to prove their existence to the intelligentsia and leave no scope for any faith, doubt or debate; then they shall only need to grasp and benefit from them. And expectedly, those who really wish to help themselves and change their life for the better will at least do as much. Only once this happens, will the entire humanity be able to scale the heights of success in life. At present, only a few who are wittingly or unwittingly living in harmony with these secret powers are able to lead a beautiful existence. The rest are just struggling in life, with troubles galore. Honestly speaking, I cannot bear to see man live in this ignominious state. I am sure, my efforts shall benefit you, and one day, the entire humanity too! Then no human being will have to dream of any heaven, rather, he will be able to create an elysian world on this earth, much more beautiful than any imaginary heaven. But remember, it takes two to tango; it cannot be a one-sided effort! I am fulfilling my duty by speaking on and writing about these secret forces. You just have to grasp and imbibe them as fast as you can and as much as you can. The rest shall fall in place automatically.

To put it succinctly, two worlds are co-existent. One is the 'visible' and the other is the 'invisible' world. A human being desires wealth, prosperity and a lot more in the visible world, but is unable to comprehend that all his desires to attain things in the visible world are ultimately aimed at experiencing joy and pleasure within i.e. in his invisible mind. In other words, even while nurturing desires and fulfilling them, his focus remains on the 'invisible'. And it is this power of the invisible that everyone must understand. It is imperative for everyone to realise that one's external life and internal life both are influenced by the 'invisible'. And if this is the case, why does one nurture all desires in the 'visible'? Why does one make all efforts in the 'visible'? Whether it is wealth, prosperity or anything else that one wishes to attain, why does one toil in the visible world? All teachings in the world including religious teachings keep encouraging one to make efforts in the visible world. But as all these teachings are basically faulty, they have miserably failed in serving the purpose of leading humans on the right path. This is the reason why in spite of incessant efforts, no one is able to achieve what they desire. Nevertheless, if you wish to build a great life for yourself, then you shall have to grasp this plain and simple truth.

In brief, one has to comprehend that the reins of everything unfolding in the visible world are in the hands of the invisible human mind and the invisible secret powers of Nature. For whatever you might wish to attain, you shall have to work in tandem with your invisible mind and the invisible secret powers of Nature. Comprehension of this basic truth is the only recourse for humanity to change their life for the better and lead a beautiful existence. And in order to translate this into reality, I have decided to pen books on the human mind and all the secret invisible powers of Nature with a scientific approach. I am sure, one day, this attempt being made with the grace of Nature shall definitely bear fruit.

Yours truly,
Deep Trivedi

/deeptrivediblog | /deeptrivediblog | /deeptrivedivideos

What is the Soul?

Your entire life is governed by the invisible powers that function according to set laws, and the 'invisible' is beyond the purview of the Brain and the Ego. The reach of the Brain and Ego is limited only to the 'visible'...and all the 'visibles' are just an illusion. That is why only the invisible i.e. the Mind can transform one's life.

This book entails a detailed discussion on '*Aatma*' or 'Soul' and all facets relating to it. Upon a little reflection, you will realise that the word 'Soul' is not new; it has been in existence since time immemorial. In spite of this, no one can answer assertively for what exactly the Soul is. There is a reason for this! Actually, human consciousness or the knowledge of human psychology is not yet evolved to a level wherefrom a common man would be able to fathom the play of the invisible, its psychology or its powers. The consciousness of a majority of people is confined to the visible world—like house, car, husband, wife, physical body, moon and stars, sea, wealth, idols, etc. Since they exist in the visible domain, they are easily comprehensible for them. But when we talk of elements beyond Time and Space, i.e. the 'invisible', one is left speechless and confounded. Whether it is the spiciness of a green chilli or the sweetness of sugar, whether it is sorrow or love, has anyone ever been able to explain any of these? Yes, we do experience these tastes and emotions, and the matter ends there. Why? This is because although the 'invisible' can be experienced, it is extremely difficult to explain it. For instance, can you ever make anyone, who has never tasted a chilli, understand what spiciness means? It is next to impossible!

Now just think, if it is impossible to make anyone understand the sweetness of sugar or the spiciness of a green chilli, how can one explain Soul, Time, God, Mind, Powers of Mind, Destiny, Automation, Energy, Time and Space Relativity, *Karma* and its fruit, birth-rebirth, etc.? Of course, the one whose consciousness continues to grow and evolve, will gradually experience all these profundities within. But even if one is asked to explain any of these, how can he possibly do it? For example, one who has never eaten a green chilli cannot be made to understand its spiciness. Similarly, one whose consciousness is not yet evolved, would never be able to comprehend anything about the Soul, the powers of the mind, destiny or the principles of Time.

In short, the invisible elements can surely be experienced, but cannot be easily comprehended or explained. Thus, if you wish to grasp the invisible powers and their secrets, then it would be prudent to bear this in mind. Instead of just trying to comprehend them, search for them in your experiences as much as possible. You must bear in mind that they cannot be grasped with mere comprehension. In fact, everyone has gone astray in their effort to comprehend them. This is the reason why, there are thousands of people today trying to explain the 'invisible' using different methods, and there are multitudes waiting to eagerly grasp these explanations as well. As a result, there are countless definitions, interpretations and explanations regarding Destiny, God and Soul, and in fact, none of these interpretations have anything in common. Ironically, most of these interpretations are far removed from the truth.

This, in turn, leads us to the question as to why the human being is so deluded in matters pertaining to the invisible powers. The reason is, he attempts to comprehend them with the help of his brain and senses, which actually is impossible. All the mysterious invisible powers can only be experienced in the awakened consciousness of the mind. So, focus all your efforts in awakening your consciousness and thereupon experience the secret powers in the awakened consciousness. Only then will you be able to fully benefit from these profound secret powers. Leave the task of comprehending these powers and debating upon them to the pseudo-intellectuals. People of their ilk have decided to lead a sorrowful existence. Leave them alone! You just focus on awakening your consciousness, experience these secret powers in it, and follow the guided path to create a great life for yourself. This is a golden opportunity for you to grasp and imbibe the mysterious powers of the mind and Nature. So, kindly do not let such an opportunity go in vain!

In a nutshell, being oblivious of the powers of one's mind, and being ignorant of the play of Nature and its secret powers is the chief cause of the sorry state of human life. Otherwise, a human being is an instrument created by Nature that can rule over the entire universe. Struggling for food, clothing and shelter, grappling with relationships and trying to survive in the world is not the life he is meant to lead. Nature's purpose behind the evolution of a great consciousness in the form of a human being, is not to make him lead a life full of perils and struggles. But, alas! What can Nature do if a human being is not able to awaken the consciousness gifted to him, and if he continues to let it lie dormant?

Hence, all must clearly understand that if one's life is fraught with pain and struggles, then the sole cause behind it is their dormant consciousness. How can Nature be blamed if the unawakened consciousness creates its own definitions and interpretations of Destiny, God, Time or Energy and proudly abides by them? How can a human being blame Destiny or God, if he himself chooses to ignore the powers of the mind bestowed upon him by Nature, and lead a painful existence?

Hence, it is essential for everyone to first comprehend the importance of awakening one's consciousness. One must realise that without awakening one's consciousness, one cannot experience any of Nature's supreme powers such as Destiny, God, Mind or Time. At this juncture, I must reiterate that all these secret forces need to be experienced, and not comprehended. The reason I am emphatically reiterating this point is, a human being, under the influence of false knowledge, gets caught in the vicious cycle of trying to comprehend them first; and then he endlessly defends and argues upon the same; and that too with such conviction as if he was the creator of all these secret powers! But of what use is such idle talk? In the end, such foolhardiness deludes him and drives him further away from the truths!

Moreover, it is imperative to realise that all these powers are not miraculous; they are all bound by their respective laws. Hence, this rules out any scope to indulge in talks of miracles or myths. Indeed, indulging in such talks and thinking tends to further mislead the human beings. In truth, there exists a complete science behind all the invisible powers. Hence, it is possible to comprehend all the laws and principles governing them. And while discussing the laws of Nature, I shall surely elucidate all these laws, secret forces and principles in depth.

Also, let me make it amply clear at this point, that my motto in whatever I speak or write, is to awaken the human consciousness. To this effect, I sometimes, target the wrong beliefs and notions, and at other times, speak of progressing on the path of consciousness. I have an in-depth understanding of both the human mind and the phenomena of Nature. I, hence, well know how to awaken the dormant human consciousness, and what and how to speak in order to fortify the deluded and corrupt human mind with various powers. Thus, whatever I speak or write is a powerful psycho-treatment that ensures the evolution of the mind and consciousness. Of course, there is no hope in the case of a person who lives in a state of deep slumber, or if his consciousness is completely dormant. If the door is slightly ajar, one can easily enter. And if the door is shut, one can kick it open i.e. use strong language to open it. And I can do both! But no sooner am I in, than some people rush to shut themselves up in their bathrooms! Now, it is against the etiquette to break open the bathroom door and invade their privacy! In such cases, even Nature feels compelled to leave these people alone, undisturbed in their respective states. So, what can I possibly do? It is these 'sleeping beauties' who are then forced to lead an existence relying on myths and miracles. People like these abound everywhere, espousing their fanatical ideas!

Well! Let such people dwell in their delusions! But, you should at least realise that even the best of medicines, at the most, can be force-fed into someone's mouth; but whether or not to gulp it down is entirely an individual, subjective call of that person. He is free to spit out even the best of medicines! So, it is up to you to decide whether or not you wish to awaken your consciousness! However, here you must bear in mind, that unless you awaken your consciousness, you will not be able to shape and transform your life. Hence, it is your responsibility to allow this new and profound knowledge to seep into your consciousness. And this is all you have to do! The rest of the task will be accomplished by the truths that I am revealing here.

Moreover, I do not stop at the mere proclamation that the Soul is immortal, or that the entire game of life is about Time, or that the mind is potent with various powers! I well know that if I state that the Soul is immortal, then the human being of the present scientific age needs to be convinced about the immortality of the Soul. As a matter of fact, the present-age human being is far more intelligent than his predecessors. Furthermore, he has access to singular scientific progress. And I am well aware that it is erroneous to presume that only the 'visible' can be proved and not the 'invisible'. I have already stated earlier that the entire functioning of Nature and life is nothing but a science. And everything that has a scientific base can always be proved. That is why, I never make a statement that cannot be proved. I am as much dedicated to the task of scientifically proving the existence of all secret powers along with the highs and lows of human life as I am to the task of awakening the human consciousness.

You just need to comprehend that the 'visible' can be tested and proved in a science laboratory, while the invisible is automatically proved in the deep recesses of an awakened human mind. Once you bear this in mind, everything will become easily comprehensible to you. And as my entire discussion revolves around the 'invisible', let my words directly find their way into the very depths of your mind. There, they will be proved automatically according to the level of the awakening of your consciousness. Do not even try to comprehend or compare these truths with the baseless notions you have heard or read so far, else you shall meander from your path and it shall render you incapable of grasping them ever. However, there is an art to instantly experience these truths too. Just do not allow what you have known, believed or understood to interfere in this process. Instead, just let these truths seep directly into the depths of your mind. For, in the depths of your mind lies supreme knowledge. It shall weigh each of these truths on its own scales and endorse them with its seal of approval.

Now let us commence our discussion on the principal subject of this book, the Soul. The usage of the term 'Soul' is quite common, but to grasp its real meaning or even explain it in its truest sense, is indeed a Herculean task for people. As a matter of fact, all the 'invisibles' are beyond the comprehension and reach of human beings; and the Soul is no exception to this. At best, most people perceive the Soul to be as a widely accepted measure of truth. And this is the reason, oftentimes, every person speaking untruth is preached to seek refuge in his Soul and pay heed to his conscience. At the same time, there are many people who associate it with ghosts and spirits, and also there are those who consider the existence of Soul as make-believe; especially, scientists, who consider the human brain as the supreme power of human existence. However, the 'invisible powers' do not fall under the purview of Science. Science functions within the parameters of Time and Space, but this does not mean that things that are beyond the reach of 'Time' and 'Space' do not exist. They do exist, and that too, in infinite numbers. The Soul is also one of them, which is firmly lodged in a human being. Simultaneously, you must also grasp that nothing in Nature is either fictitious or suppositious. Everything in existence is lawfully governed and it is only because of these laws that they have come to exist. The only difference is, the invisible powers have always been the subject of spiritual science. In fact, everything I speak or write pertains to spiritual science. This is the reason all the invisible powers of human beings and Nature have always been the main subjects of interest for me. And on that basis, I would like to make it clear that the Soul was, is and will always be the ultimate power bestowed upon a human being by Nature; this is the very design of Nature for a human being. Unfortunately, despite this fact, by and large, the human being lives in ignorance of the Soul. Hence, my motive behind penning this book is to introduce you to your Soul and aid you to not only enter the realm of the Soul but also anchor yourself in it. Indubitably, it is difficult to comprehend as well as explain the Soul, even so, I shall, in a lucid manner, endeavour to give you an in-depth explanation of the Soul so that it becomes easy for you to grasp it. Nevertheless, before we tread on this journey, you shall have to, first and foremost, recognise yourself fully and comprehend the complex structure of a human being. Thus, in this book, my foremost attempt will be to introduce you to your true self. At the same time, I shall also discuss everything that Krishna has enunciated in the Gita with reference to the Soul. This is of utmost significance because Krishna is the first person to elucidate the workings of the Soul in such detail. Once you recognise yourself and grasp the Soul as described by Krishna, I shall give you a detailed explanation of the Soul with a scientific approach, and in the process help you experience and realise your Soul too. The only cooperation I seek from you is to allow everything I say to seep into the depths of your mind. It is my promise, once you realise your Soul, your life will scale unprecedented heights of joy!

Therefore, I now hope that you are ready to experience the Soul and its powers, draw maximum benefit from them and lay the foundation of a great life ahead. It will gratify me extremely if you make the most of this opportunity and not let this chance of experiencing the Soul go in vain.

The Relation between Krishna and the Soul

Attainment of self-realisation by suppressing the mind, brain, ego and body is not a great feat, but aligning them with the Soul surely is. And Krishna teaches us to accomplish this remarkable feat.

While speaking of the Soul, it becomes pertinent to speak of Krishna. For, Krishna is the first person in human history to use the word *Aatma* (Soul) several times in the Bhagavad Gita—an epitome of wisdom enunciated by him. In this epic text, he has elucidated the powers and the influences of the Soul in many different ways. And Krishna is not one to indulge in empty talk. Anything he states stems directly from his experience. In fact, it is an integral part of his life and he very well lived in it. Krishna not only possesses a deep understanding of the play of Nature and the powers of the human mind, but he also comprehends the significance of maintaining harmony between these two. This is the reason why he never lost any battle of his life and in fact, the savants have eulogised him as the complete man or *Purna Avatar* in the history of human race. This indeed is an unchallengeable truth that one does not have a reason to counter or deny.

Nevertheless, one must always remember that great people do not belong to any religion or society; they belong to the entire humanity. In fact, the practice of society and religion to exert exclusive right over them has only caused grave loss to mankind. Hence, the sensible and wise ones who wish to lead a great life should free themselves of such absurdities. Therefore, do not ever get into an idiosyncrasy such as, "Why is my God lesser than yours in any way or why is your God greater?", otherwise you shall certainly digress from the path. If Krishna is a multidimensional and multitalented personality, then he sure is. But this does not mean, he is a magician or a mythical character. Know it with certainty that if you consider Krishna to be a miracle worker, then you shall not only miss the bus but also deviate from your path. Factually speaking, what makes Krishna a man of substance is his charismatic personality and his treasure trove of talent. Otherwise, akin to us, he, too was born on this earth and all the secret laws of the universe were equally applicable to him as much as they are applicable to us. However, many people, propelled by their ignorance, self-centeredness, ego and the desire for their trade in religion to flourish, have projected Krishna as a magical or mythical character. Although, the ancient texts reveal the facts about the entire life and actual personality of Krishna, unfortunately, these texts are rarely discussed. Instead, spurious texts which were written to curb the rising influence of Buddhism are much widely discussed and more in vogue.

You must all be aware of the period when Hindus, attracted by Buddha's charisma, were making a beeline to convert to Buddhism. It was during this time that a few fictitious texts were written to curb the influence of Buddha and these texts portrayed Krishna as a magical and mythical person, interpolating his life with wondrous miracles. The common folk as well as those trading in religion were fascinated by this new 'avatar' of Krishna. But this also had a downside; the conscientious humans with scientific intelligence could not accept this form of Krishna and they distanced themselves from it. If analysed minutely, one would realise that what transpired thereafter was not right. In fact, these fictitious texts had two negative impacts. Firstly, those who were gullible enough to become enamoured by this new miracle-working Krishna not only lost their way, but were also cheated and looted by those who propagated stories of the magical acts of Krishna; and unfortunately, this loot is prevalent even today. And secondly, the aware humans who could have grasped Krishna, in the truest sense, and performed great deeds for the collective good, distanced themselves from Krishna. Had they retained their interest in Krishna, today, the list of great people would have been much longer. We are all well aware that the endeavours of every great person help in making the lives of millions successful. And the phenomenal progress achieved by humanity so far is attributed to these great people. The poor common man, in spite of taking advantage of their great achievements, is still struggling in life just because of his unawakened consciousness. Just imagine the state of humanity, had these great people not existed! Hence, the importance of great persons in our lives is priceless and undeniable. Just think, had Krishna not been metamorphosed into a larger-than-life character, wouldn't the intelligentsia have benefitted from his real life and knowledge, and attained greatness themselves? And if the percentage of great people in this world had increased, wouldn't this world have been a better and more beautiful place for all of us to live in?

However, let bygones be bygones! Currently, let us talk about the personality of the real Krishna and not the magical character that people in general assume. And the actual, great Krishna was not just the first psychologist, rather, he was the first scientist in the history of human race. He is the one whose consciousness had scaled unprecedented heights. In spite of all this, let me make it amply clear that as a human being, he led a life with all the limitations that bind human life and human body. The limitations that are applicable to human beings in general, were equally applicable to him too. For example, when shot by an arrow in the foot, Krishna too breathed his last. But most importantly, in spite of having taken birth in a dungeon, he attained extraordinary heights. However, that was the accomplishment of his consciousness and not any miracle. One who comprehends Krishna's life in view of the above-stated facts, will know whatever there is to be known, and will learn whatever there is to be learnt. And he shall experience not just the Soul and God within, rather, he shall experience within all the other plays of Nature too. Thereupon, he will become as invincible and great as Krishna, and never lose any battle in his life. On the basis of my experiences, I can emphatically state that humanity has no treasure as valuable and great as the life of Krishna and the Bhagavad Gita enunciated by him. But unfortunately, man has failed to grasp both and benefit from them.

In simple words, Bhagavad Gita is the account of how an ordinary boy, Krishna, born in a dungeon, transformed to become the all-hailed Jai Sri Krishna. That is why, the Gita is called the formula for success.

But benefit we will! I want the entire world to benefit from the journey of Krishna's transformation, success and progress in life. It is with this purpose that I have penned the book 'I am Krishna' that entails the life of Krishna, the evolution of his mind and psychology, how he established a harmony with all the powers of Nature and how he transformed from a little boy named *Kanha* to become the all-hailed – *Jai Shri Krishna*! I have penned this book after having thoroughly researched all the authentic and available ancient texts. It is a labour of love spanning six volumes and has been penned in great detail, delving deep into every psychological evolution of his life. I have written about Krishna's life in great depth because I know and I am conversant with the importance of his life, mind, accomplishments, powers, capabilities and his ability to align himself with Nature and progress in life. This biography of Krishna certainly has the potential of changing the destiny of the entire humanity. This is because Krishna's life not only teaches us how to save ourselves from falling prey to the dangerous ideas germinating out of the chaotic human mind, rather, it also instructs us as to how to take advantage of the law-bound, complicated powers of Nature. And I don't think there can be any knowledge more important than this in the world.

Let me also highlight this point here that while writing the biography of Krishna, I have ignored all fictitious texts written on Krishna in the past 1000 years because their portrayal of Krishna has nothing in common with the real Krishna. In fact, fools, in their race to prove their God a greater miracle worker, and selfish ones, to run their trade in religion, have mythologised the life of great people to an extent that it has floundered and veered away from the real truth. And this is the case with not just Krishna's life but also the lives of all the great people such as Buddha, Christ, Kabir and Meera. It is just because the so-called savants have misrepresented the life stories of great people that humanity is till date stumbling in darkness. Hence, only those, who are able to grasp the ground reality that all great people were born on this very earth and were governed by the same existential laws of Nature, shall be able to benefit from their lives and teachings. The rest shall continue to harp on fictitious stories, believing them to be the gospel truth. Indeed, these people will continue to be victimised in the name of religion and continue to frequent their respective religious places such as temples, churches and mosques that are all a part of the nexus that loots in the name of these great people.

In brief, whether it is the play of Nature or that of human life, everything is scientifically bound by laws, which can not only be experienced but also proved. Hence, myths and miracles have no place in any of Nature's truths. I am emphatically reiterating this point because the factual lives of Krishna, Buddha, Christ, Kabir and Meera provide us with a glimpse of not just the Soul but also its various powers. And I wish for mankind to benefit from it. That is why in the introduction to this book I have discussed these great people, especially Krishna in such detail. Further, I shall explain all that Krishna has enunciated about the Soul and its powers in the Bhagavad Gita. I am sure, the elucidation of the Soul by Krishna will lay a strong foundation for you to understand what the Soul actually is!

Importance of the Bhagavad Gita

The very significance
of the Bhagavad Gita lies in the fact
that Arjuna leaves no scope for Krishna
to feel the absence of anyone to counter him.
He is already expressing all the doubts
that can possibly be expressed
to counter Krishna.

Having understood several aspects of Krishna's life, now we shall endeavour to grasp the importance of the Bhagavad Gita because all that he has spoken about the Soul is contained in the Gita. Hence, it is imperative to understand what the Bhagavad Gita is all about. To begin with, the Bhagavad Gita is a complete scripture in itself. Whether one wants to comprehend human life or the secret forces of Nature, whether one wants to awaken one's consciousness or realise one's duties, the Bhagavad

Gita is unparalleled in all cases. Right from the problems of daily life to the realisation of the Supreme Knowledge, Krishna has spoken about everything in detail in the Gita. Moreover, in the Gita, Krishna has also elucidated the difference between those who are religious and those who are irreligious. Additionally, the elucidation of the three-dimensional theory in the Bhagavad Gita makes it a cut above the rest of the scriptures. Besides, the Bhagavad Gita is a psychological scripture that contains the saga of the entire psychological duel between Krishna and Arjuna. Indeed, the psychological exchange in the form of dialogue that goes on between them for eighteen chapters is capable of making humanity transcend newer psychological heights. Moreover, this psychological exchange between the two also explains how one can vanquish the struggles of daily life.

Nevertheless, we are all aware of what the youth stands to achieve after spending twenty years in academic education. And we are also aware of what one gains by visiting religious places such as temples, mosques and churches for years. In view of the above-stated facts, I can assertively state that if a human being were to devote just five per cent of the focus and time that he spends in schools and religious places in trying to understand the Bhagavad Gita, then his life would scale unprecedented, phenomenal heights. This is why, ideally, the Bhagavad Gita should be made a part of the school curriculum. Only then will every human being be able to extract maximum advantage from his studies, skills and talents. As it is the eternal truth of life, that one with a weak psychology can neither reap benefits of his talents nor of his academic qualifications.

Therefore, one must grasp and realise the significance of the Bhagavad Gita, for it is not a scripture meant only for the Hindus. In fact, in the entire Bhagavad Gita, Krishna has not even once used the word ‘Hindu’. Well, a man like Krishna can never stoop so low to think in such a prudish manner. The Gita enunciated by Krishna is above all religions. Hence, everyone should get rid of their narrow-mindedness and accept the Bhagavad Gita as a Universal Scripture. Only then shall we be able to change the prevalent scenario and transform the face and fate of this world. As I well know the significance of the Bhagavad Gita, to achieve this, I have delivered 168 hours of lectures on the Gita containing the elucidation of all 700 verses, which is a record by itself.

However, our current topic of discussion is not the details of the Gita, but the description of the Soul and its influences on which Krishna sheds light in the Gita. Hence, I shall describe the Soul on the basis of a few verses from the Gita that will surely help you get a glimpse of the Soul.

1

Bhagavad Gita, Chapter 2, Verses 20-25

Krishna: This Soul is never born nor it ever dies; neither does it rise again nor can it come into being. For, it is unborn, eternal, everlasting and primeval; even though the body is slain, the Soul is not. ||20||

O Arjuna, son of Pritha! How can one who knows this Soul to be imperishable, eternal and free from birth and decay—kill or cause someone to be killed? ||21||

As a man sheds worn-out garments and dons other new ones, the embodied Soul, casting off worn-out bodies, enters into others that are new. ||22||

Weapons cannot cut the Soul, nor can fire burn it; water cannot wet it, nor can wind dry it. ||23||

For, this Soul cannot be cut, burnt, drenched or dried; this Soul is eternal, omnipresent, immovable, constant and primeval. ||24||

This Soul is unmanifest, inconceivable and this Soul is said to be free of Vikaaras (deformities, defects and disorders). Hence, O Arjuna! Knowing the Soul thus, there is no cause for you to mourn. In other words, it is not right on your part to grieve. ||25||

In fact, if one were to delve into the depths of the Bhagavad Gita, and make an attempt to decipher the profound meaning of Krishna's words, then one could write tomes on each verse and speak for hours at length. However, this is a book about the Soul and not about the Bhagavad Gita. Therefore, without deviating from the topic, I shall focus my discussions on interpreting the meaning of a few verses of the Gita, majorly elucidating the Soul.

But firstly, one must bear in mind that Krishna is enunciating the Bhagavad Gita to Arjuna, and not to you or me. In my experience, most of us who read or try to explain the Gita tend to ignore this very fact. Instead, they immediately attempt to decipher these verses in their subjective context which tends to distort their very meaning and leads to misinterpretation. The Gita does not contain 700 individual verses, rather it is a scripture of 700 verses seamlessly interconnected with each other. It begins with Arjuna's imbalanced state of mind and progresses according to the changing state of his mind, from moment to moment. Hence, it would be prudent of you to bear in mind that whenever and whatever wisdom Krishna enunciates correlates to Arjuna's state of mind at that particular moment. Thus, in order to fathom the intricate meaning of any verse of the Gita, one has to first understand Arjuna's state of mind prior to the utterance of that particular verse. This is the reason my 168-hours-long lectures on the Gita explains all the 700 verses one after another in great detail. And before elucidating each of the verses, I have inevitably expounded upon the state of Arjuna's mind at that moment. This is the only way of comprehending the complete psychological depth of the Bhagavad Gita.

Therefore, please beware of those who make ludicrous interpretations of the Gita. Instead, read it based on the premise I have just shared with you, and it will create a greater impact. As the Gita speaks of human life, any person reading it with a bit of awareness, will well be able to decipher it and grasp it. One must also bear in mind that Krishna led an all-encompassing, complete life. Hence, whether it is the Gita or the life of Krishna, only he, who can accept life in its totality, in all its shades, can grasp them in depth. Otherwise, know it for sure that those who take the path of escapism by way of renunciation or those who accord importance to such beliefs, will neither be able to comprehend the Gita nor the life of Krishna. Also, those who are under the influence of other religious texts will never be able to understand the Gita, and will flounder till their last breath, even if such influence comes from the Hindu religion. But as I have already mentioned, the Bhagavad Gita unveils the profound secrets of both the human life and Nature. That is why, the Bhagavad Gita is the only medium through which one can comprehend the heights of human life or Nature.

Nevertheless, presently, let us return to the above mentioned verses enunciated by Krishna. Both you and I shall have to bear in mind that this book is about the Soul and not the Gita. Hence, so far, I have explained all that was essential to understand the Gita and Krishna. Now, we shall begin with the first of the verses mentioned above in relation to the Soul. In this verse, Krishna elucidates the immortality of the Soul. He says, "O Arjuna, you are the Soul, I am the Soul and so are these kings. And Soul is indestructible; it neither takes birth, nor does it die." That is, the Soul is neither born, nor does it ever get destroyed. Hence, the question of anyone dying just does not arise. And when no one can die, there arises no question of killing anyone either. In truth, no one ever dies and no one can ever be killed. To speak of dying and killing is proof of being caught in the vortex of delusion of this physical world. In reality, these things are simply non-existent.

This, in turn, gives rise to the question, 'Why is Krishna explaining this to Arjuna?' Indeed, Krishna is not one to expend his time and energy in pointless pursuits. Hence, you must bear in mind the purpose with which Krishna is explaining all this; because at the moment Arjuna is not only frightened, but also confused. He is worried about the outcome of the war. 'Will I be killed?' 'Will I be the slayer of my brothers, uncles and teachers?' Arjuna feels, whether he is killed or he kills his brothers and relatives, grief is

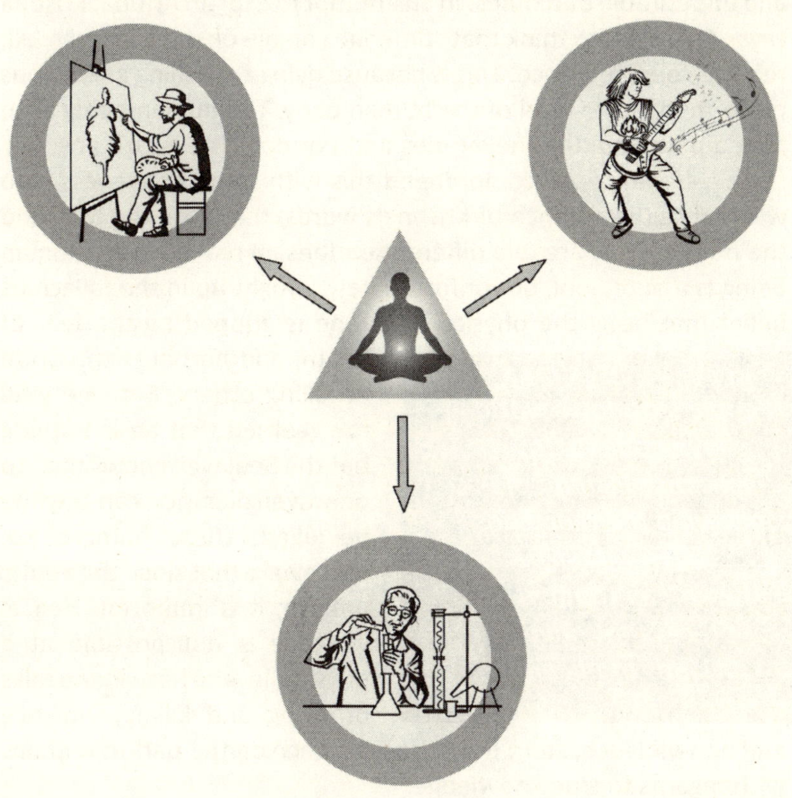

Virtue of Soul

Happiness, joy, peace, concentration, creativity and intelligence are all attributes of the Soul. If you don't have these qualities, know with certainty that you are distanced from your Soul.

ascertained in both the cases. Thus, he feels both would be wrong and undesirable outcomes. In an attempt to explain Arjuna, Krishna says, 'O Arjuna, to think that someone can die or someone can kill, reflects your ignorance. This is because dying and killing are actions performed at the level of the human body. The human being is, in fact, a pure Soul that never dies and nor does it ever kill anyone.'

If you try to comprehend this with some awareness, you will realise the essence of Krishna's words, that both the Soul and the human body are two different entities. In reality, every human being is a pure Soul, but unfortunately, caught up in the fallacious belief that he is the physical body, he is gripped by the fear of death, and harbours the pride of killing others. But one who has realised that he is nothing but the Soul well knows that no one ever dies nor can anyone be killed. These humans are also aware that since the Soul is unborn, it is immortal. Hence, violence is not possible at a physical level. These inane talks of dying and killing, violence and non-violence, stem from the ignorance on the part of humans with regards to true knowledge.

People in today's world have gone astray because instead of following the teachings of wise men, they are entangled in scriptures that advocate all kinds of idiocies.

A deeper understanding of the immortality of the Soul will make you realise that Krishna, by saying thus, is trying to lift the veil off all talks prevalent in the world regarding dying and killing, violence and non-violence, as it is a convoluted way of thinking of the so-called intellects who consider the physical form as real. It does not really matter whether such fallacious thinking is being propounded by any religion or by a person considered an erudite on the subject. One must realise that Krishna is speaking the ultimate truth. When it comes to the ultimate truth or the secret forces of Nature, all baseless knowledge that has been heard or read, bites the dust. And the ultimate truth of this universe is, no one ever dies and no one can ever be killed. Here, one should also bear in mind that superficial knowledge might grant temporary relief, but if one desires permanent solace, then one has no option but to live in harmony with the secret forces of Nature. Hence, on delving deeper, one would realise what Krishna is explaining to Arjuna, that both birth and death are delusions. And till the time one harbours this delusion, one will have to bear the grief of birth and death. If one desires to get rid of this grief permanently, then one has no option but to live in the realisation of the immortality of the Soul.

Indeed, as I have spoken at such length on this subject, I would also like to state that Krishna is the greatest exponent of non-violence. What non-violence truly means, can best be understood only from Krishna's life and through the Gita elucidated by him. Seemingly, the common belief that Krishna slayed many people in his life, or he caused the war of Mahabharata and Yadavasthali, which culminated in the massacre of innumerable lives, has been formed due to ignorance on the part of people. However, let me emphatically state, that this is the result of having a parochial mentality...which is beyond comprehension. I only want to state that the secret forces of Nature are truly profound. If you try to assess them on the basis of your limiting beliefs or the false knowledge propagated by ignorant beings, you will never be able to comprehend anything, instead you shall aimlessly wander forever.

As for the present, it is sufficient for you to know and be content in the fact that you and I both are Souls; and the Soul neither dies nor can it kill anyone. Only ignorant beings who consider themselves to be physical forms and not the Soul, adopt thoughts and beliefs contrary to this truth and remain aggrieved. Hence, discard all false notions, and realise yourself to be the Soul as soon as possible and as much as you can. Lest, like Arjuna, you too, will become prey to the grief of the notions of dying and killing on a regular basis.

2

Bhagavad Gita, Chapter 3, Verses 17-18

Krishna: O Arjuna, the human being, who takes delight in the Soul, who is gratified with the Soul and is contented in the Soul alone, has no duty to perform. ||17||

In this world, that great Soul has no impetus for action nor for abstaining from action. He has no selfish interest in his relations with any creature. ||18||

This is indeed a profound verse enunciated by Krishna. Prior to the enunciation of this verse, Arjuna refers to the scriptures and says – 'O Krishna! It is mentioned in the scriptures that the one who slays his brothers and teachers not only rots in hell, rather, his misdeed spells doom for his entire clan. It does not behove me to commit such a sin for the sake of a kingdom.' Having spoken thus, Arjuna asks Krishna to enlighten him about the characteristics of a *SiddhPurush* (enlightened person). Arjuna says – 'I feel confused and I am caught in the vortex between what you say and that which is stated in the scriptures. While the scriptures mention that killing is a sin, you state that sin and virtue are merely delusions of the human mind.' Thus, the above verses have been enunciated by Krishna for Arjuna, whose mind at that moment is deluded and assailed with doubts.

As I have stated earlier, the Gita is a dialogue between two people. Hence, before attempting to interpret the verses, it is imperative to first understand Arjuna's state of mind at the specific moment and use that as a premise to understand the questions he puts forth to Krishna. Throughout the course of the Gita, Arjuna's state of mind changes with each passing moment. That is why, the answers given by Krishna also keep changing along with Arjuna's changing state of mind, and there are several instances in the Gita when Krishna is perforced to retract his own words. Unfortunately, those who lack the knowledge of psychology construe these statements as contradictory. But it is not so! It may seem that Krishna is contradicting himself, but if you carefully decipher it in the context of Arjuna's changing state of mind, you will realise that the advice that Krishna gives to Arjuna is relevant at that particular moment in time. That is, both the statements perceived as contradictory hold true in their respective context in view of Arjuna's changing state of mind. Therefore, never search for any contradiction in the words of Krishna, or for that matter, of any wise person. If you wish to fathom the depths of a statement, you need to first consider the circumstances under which the statement has been made. Else, like other misguided people, you too will flounder and veer away from the truth.

Having said that, it is but natural for Arjuna to be confused between what Krishna is saying and that which is mentioned in the scriptures. As it is obvious that Krishna's verses will not match with what the scriptures preach. And interestingly, the difference between the two lies in the innate psychology that each propounds. While the scriptures indulge in idle talk, Krishna only speaks of the Eternal Truth. The main focus of the scriptures is propagation of its beliefs, whereas Krishna is focussed on human upliftment. He does not seek any *Guru Dakshina* (fee) from Arjuna or aim to establish any *Ashram* (hermitage). Hence, it is well-nigh impossible for the twain to meet - the words of the scriptures and those of Krishna's. Moreover, Krishna also understands Arjuna's confused state of mind, torn as he is between the contradictory statements propounded by the scriptures and those espoused by him. And when Arjuna enquires about the characteristics of an enlightened person (*SiddhPurush*), Krishna immediately grabs this chance to explain his stance to Arjuna. He feels that while answering this question, he would easily be able to pull Arjuna out of the influence of the so-called scriptures. Elucidating the characteristics of an enlightened person, Krishna well explains to Arjuna, that such a person leads his life, not by following the scriptures, but by heeding the voice of his Soul. Krishna states that such a person dwells in the Soul and acts only by the Soul and remains contented in it. For him, his very 'being' is enough and complete in itself. He feels so content with just the experience of his 'being', that he harbours no other desires. And when there is no desire, there is no cause or aim behind his actions too. In a nutshell, Krishna says, "O Arjuna, unlike you, an enlightened person would never take recourse to the scriptures and consider not going to war as the best course of action. Procrastinating or abstaining from an action that ought to be done, due to the fear of hell or the anxiety of the loss of one's clan, is definitely not the trait of an enlightened person. An enlightened person performs every action that stems from his Soul naturally, without any greed or fear. O Arjuna, understand well that as the enlightened being has no selfish interest in any being, he is not bound by any duty too. He just effortlessly performs every action that ought to be done. Thereupon, he does not worry about the results, consequences or loss or gain while performing that action. O Arjuna, the Soul functions with the sole realisation that an action that ought to be performed, must be performed at any cost, and an action that must not be performed, must not be performed under any circumstances. In such a case, where does the question of pondering upon virtue-sin, gain-loss, good-bad, success-failure or any such baseless notions arise? Only the ignorant beings, who perceive the physical form as real, give importance to such notions. That is why, they weigh their actions on the scales of virtue-sin, good-bad and gain-loss. And unfortunately, Arjuna, you too are doing the same at present. You are weighing your decision of going or not going to war on numerous scales such as virtue-sin and gain-loss. This is the reason why you have become completely deluded and confused right now, while an enlightened being is never confused about anything. For such wise beings, what ought to be done, ought to be done. And once they have done it, the matter ends there. They are then not worried about heaven or hell, virtue or sin. Hence, you should understand that if the war of Mahabharata has to take place, then it surely will. What can you or I do in such an eventuality? During such imminent events, only ignorant ones who are brimming with ego and are deluded into thinking that they are greater than Nature, speak of virtue and sin. And it is these ignorant people who speak of changing or altering the course of naturally occurring events of Nature or escaping them. Dear readers, if you carefully grasp, then this one verse is enough to banish a thousand delusions and confusions in life. Therefore, you must try to take maximum possible advantage of these words of Krishna. Do not let a single chance of moving closer to your Soul go in vain. Believe me, the closer you move to your Soul, the more you shall be imbued with supreme powers.

3

Bhagavad Gita, Chapter 4, Verse 24

In the practice of seeing Brahma everywhere as a form of sacrifice, Brahma is the ladle (with which oblation is poured into the fire); Brahma, again, is the oblation; Brahma is the fire; Brahma itself is the sacrifice and Brahma itself is the act of pouring the oblation into the fire; and so, Brahma is the goal worth attaining for the yogi who is absorbed in Brahma as the act of such sacrifice. ||24||

Arjuna is repeatedly speaking in terms of yours and mine, one's own and others. He is worried about winning and losing, dying and killing. That is why Krishna tries to explain to him by saying, "O Arjuna, if *Yagya* or any action in life in which the doer is the Soul, the person before whom the action takes place is also the Soul, and all the resources used for performing that action are also the Soul, then the fruit of the action performed with such understanding is nothing but the joy gained from realisation of the Soul. But since you have assumed yourself to be Arjuna, those standing before you as armies of enemies and the instruments used in the warfare as weapons, you are indulging in such inane and futile talks of winning-losing, dying-killing and virtue-sin. And you too are enduring the pain and grief of such naïve thinking. But know with certainty, that in truth, no difference or distinction exists here. Perceiving a difference is in itself a proof of ignorance. In reality, everything here is the manifestation of the Soul; all human beings are nothing but Souls. And it does not matter, for how long or in what manner the Souls play with each other. Hence, there is absolutely no need for you to become serious!"

Omnipresence of Soul implies, 'there is no difference between 'me' and others.' If you perceive a difference, then your Soul is in a deep slumber.

"In short, Arjuna, till a human being perceives every individual and every element as different, he will continue to unnecessarily endure enormous mental stress. As long as humans subscribe to different religions and adhere to them with a sense of belonging, a human being will remain deluded. Till a human differentiates between acts such as worshipping God and eating, he will remain mired in problems. Look at me! Have I ever made a distinction between performing *raasa* (dancing with abandon) and war? Have I ever considered enunciation of the Gita as sacred and the war of Mahabharata as deplorable? I derive great spiritual joy in partaking of *chappanbhog* (meal of 56 delicacies), just as I do in slaying someone, as and when the need arises. I like dancing and playing the flute as much as I like wielding weapons such as a mace and my discus. This is because for an enlightened person like me, everything here is nothing but the manifestation of the Soul. Hence, you must know that all the scriptures that you refer to, for creating so many distinctions, are nothing but books filled with ignorance. Everything is the Soul and this is the only true knowledge."

4

Bhagavad Gita, Chapter 5, Verse 24

Krishna: O Arjuna, He who is happy within himself, enjoys within himself the delight of the Soul, and is also illumined by the inner light (light of the Soul), such a yogi (sankhyayogi) identified with Brahma attains Brahma, who is all peace. ||24||

After all the discussions, explanations and elucidations so far, you must have got a fair idea of how the Gita was woven into eighteen chapters. At the same time, you must have also understood that in order to comprehend the Gita, it becomes equally imperative to understand the questions posed by Arjuna as it is to decipher the answers given by Krishna. However, this book is not about the Bhagavad Gita. Hence, I will decipher these verses only in brief and will limit my elucidations to focus only on the Soul.

In this verse, Krishna states that the one who realises oneself as the Soul, no longer depends on anything in the outside world. His happiness and joy lie in the Soul alone and so do his ventures. Such a person draws all his knowledge from the Soul itself. Then, he does not bother about what has been stated by someone else. Coming to the interpretation of the verse, Krishna says, "Arjuna! I, too have heard the scriptures you are referring to. The only difference is, I give importance to the realisation of the Soul, while you give importance to the scriptures. However, it would be prudent of you to kindle self-awareness. As soon as it is awakened, you shall be free of everything propounded by the scriptures. And as soon as you are liberated of them, all your delusions shall disappear too."

"O Arjuna, you must grasp this universal truth, that everything is the Soul; this is the only true self-realisation. For such a self-enlightened person, what can be gained or lost? For him, if he gains something, it is but his Soul, and even if he loses something, it is his Soul. For such a supreme knower, the world is a stage, and all his acts and actions in the outside world are nothing but a drama. Indeed, for the ignorant ones, he may seem to be performing many actions, but for the supreme knower, those are mere acts that he performs while remaining firmly anchored in the Soul. Hence, O Arjuna, all my actions are mere acts (in the play) that I perform—be it the *Raasleela*, my love affairs, fighting, killing or gorging on the sumptuous *chappanbhog*, dancing, taking the cows for grazing or my ascension as the King of Dwarka and leading a royal life. Even while performing all these actions, I remain focussed and anchored in my Soul with the thought of oneness. You just consider this war an act of drama and play along. Do not become seriously involved in it. Instead, remain anchored in your Soul and fight the war. Then the war will no longer be a war for you, rather it will provide you the joy of *Maharaas* (a great *raasa* dance)."

5

Bhagavad Gita, Chapter 6, Verse 7

Krishna: The Supreme Spirit is rooted in the self-contained man whose mind is perfectly serene in the midst of dualities such as cold and heat, joy and sorrow, and honour and ignominy. In other words, his knowledge contains nothing but the Supreme Soul. ||7||

In this verse, Krishna elucidates a very plain and simple, yet beautiful point. He says, "O Arjuna, ups and downs are all part and parcel of life, and so are good and bad days. This is what life is all about. At the same time, it is the way of the world to honour and dishonour others at the slightest instance. Hence, all this is bound to happen in life. Look at my own life! I have always been surrounded by one problem or the other. And insults! I have faced ignominy at every step. So, should I be perturbed by all this? Should I become anxious and let the barbs affect me? Not a chance...For,

I well know that I am the pure, pristine Soul. I am not the physical form that ignorant people have identified as Krishna. Therefore, irrespective of what life offers me, it doesn't make any difference to me. These illusions are just temporary phenomena of life that hold no significance to me. I have always known my inner life driven by the Soul to be different from my physical life surrounded by worldly illusions. This is the reason, irrespective of the events unfolding in my life, I have always remained at the pinnacle of joy and happiness, leaving all these worldly impediments aside.

Hence, do not take this war, or the possibility of victory or defeat, seriously. All this is a mere game of life. Play it like a game and enjoy it. Why are you suffering by unnecessarily pondering over these inconsequential issues? Rise above these petty thoughts, and realise your existence as the Soul! You must understand that till you don't realise yourself as the Soul, you will continue to think of yourself as Arjuna. And as long as you assume yourself as Arjuna, you will find yourself caught in a whirlpool of problems and dilemmas." In a nutshell, whether it is Arjuna or you, problems in life shall continue to hound you till the time you accord greater importance to worldly matters rather than your Soul.

6

Bhagavad Gita, Chapter 10, Verse 20

Krishna: Arjuna, I am the Universal Self dwelling in the hearts of all beings; and I alone am the beginning, middle and end of all the beings. ||20||

In this verse, Krishna unveils a profound truth by explaining to Arjuna that the Soul does not exist in him alone. He says, "O Arjuna, like me, the Soul exists in you too. And not just you, I, in the form of the Soul, dwell in the hearts of all. There is no human being in whom I am not present in totality. But O Arjuna, I would like to clarify here that my presence is not limited to the hearts of human beings. Omnipresence is another facet of my Soul. Thus,

I am equally present in all the visible and invisible spectrums of this universe. Indeed, not just the past, but the present and the future of all living beings, is but a fraction of my omnipresent Soul. Thus, finding faults in any aspect of life—a situation, form or circumstance—is an insult to me (The Supreme Soul). Trust me when I tell you that the Soul is all-pervading; everything in existence is but the Soul, no matter what it is or where it is. Even this war is not an exception to this truth.

Hence, your act of finding faults in the impending war, wittingly or unwittingly, is nothing but an insult to this very Supreme Soul. But those who are aware that everything is one-Soul, do not behave in this manner. This warped human thinking of finding several faults in himself and life, stems from the notion that he exists only at a physical level. The teachings that he has imbibed from the outside world induce nothing but desires, lust, fears and ignorance and lead him to believe that he is mired in problems. For instance, at present, you feel you are stuck in the battlefield. But actually, there is no cause for concern. It is because you consider yourself to be Arjuna that you believe, you are trapped in this battle. But trust me, this war is a part of the omnipresent existence of Soul and I am very well a part of it. Hence, deserting this battlefield would mean abandoning me. And everyone is bound to bear the adverse consequences of abandoning me."

7

Bhagavad Gita, Chapter 13, Verse 22

Krishna: The Soul dwelling in the body is really the same as the Supreme Soul. He has been spoken of as witness, the true guide, the sustainer of all, the experiencer (as the embodied Soul), the overlord and the absolute as well. ||22||

In this verse, Krishna is discussing with Arjuna the delusion that occurs with respect to actions. Krishna explains that everyone is always in a state of flux regarding the course of action that is required of them, that is, which actions to indulge in and which to refrain from. This is because a human being wants to choose his actions based on the parameters of his brain and ego. But those who are aware and seekers of the Soul do not engage in such foolhardiness. They always flow in sync with the happening of Nature. Their actions are either spontaneous or are a part of the beautiful happening of Nature. There is no third cause which propels an emancipated Soul to perform an action. Their actions are never based on parameters such as virtue-sin, gain-loss and mine-yours. Hence, even while performing an action, they remain a mere witness, an observer of the action that is being performed. In other words, even while doing everything, they are actually doing nothing. They are just a spectator of their own actions and that of others; all they do is behold! This is the reason why they are never confused about any act or action. All their actions always flow forth with absolute firmness, devoid of any confusion.

Happiness and sorrow, as a whole, exist. But in this world, there is no place for individual happiness i.e. 'my' happiness and 'your' happiness.

Krishna says, "Arjuna, you too must stand your ground firmly in all circumstances and situations. But you are not able to do so. For instance, in the present war, because of your own convoluted thinking, you find yourself at a crossroads, unable to decide the right course of action for yourself. There are so many thoughts clouding your mind. But look at me! I stand firm in the battlefield, smiling, without an iota of doubt shrouding my thinking. I have no confusion at all. Why? Because I know that this war has stemmed from the flowing stream of happening of Nature; hence, there is nothing wrong in it. And the omnipotent Soul is one that sustains and nurtures one and all. Therefore, no matter how an ordinary human being perceives this war and its consequences,

I know for certain, that the end result of this war is bound to be good. If not today, its far-reaching positive results will be evident in the future."

"Arjuna, the problem is, while the ignorant human being, living in the delusion of being a physical form, becomes perturbed time and again on perceiving the immediate harms caused by an action, the knower of the Soul is clairvoyant enough to see the far-reaching benefits of his actions. Hence, have faith in your Soul, for it will make you a witness of this war. Then you will not need to think or comprehend anything; for, then you will be able to fight the war with due firmness and conviction, without any confusion. And thus, having surrendered to the Soul, in the end, like me, you too shall be a mere beholder of the war even while fighting in it."

8

Bhagavad Gita, Chapter 13, Verse 33

Krishna: O Arjuna, just as one sun illumines the entire universe, one Soul illumines the whole Kshetra (field). ||33||

In this verse, Krishna is discussing the ultimate form of the Soul. He has already revealed that the Soul is present in the heart of all beings. Also, he has stated that no particle exists in the universe which is devoid of the Soul. Now, he is stating, "Although everyone has an individual Soul, in actuality, it is just one Soul that is present in all. Just as one sun lights up the entire world, similarly, it is one Soul that is omnipresent i.e. everything in existence is the manifestation of just one Soul. Hence, do not think that everyone's Soul differs from one another. This is the perception of those who live in 'ego' rather than the 'Soul'. And as they believe in the individuality of Soul, they recognise their Soul as an individual entity and become selfish. And then propelled by their selfishness, they tend to differentiate and perceive 'my' happiness and 'your' happiness as separate. Whereas, for the one living with the realisation of oneness of the Soul, happiness is just happiness; then whether it is his own, or someone else's. He experiences within himself the happiness experienced by every human being."

"In other words, O Arjuna, while an egoist is happy with his own happiness, the seeker of the Soul is overjoyed by the happiness of every human being. Hence, do not perceive this war as a fight for victory or defeat between the Pandavas and Kauravas. This is a collective war, of which you too are a part. Similarly, you are but a part of all the warriors too; you are not separate from them. Whether it is Duryodhana or Drona, you are a part of everybody. It is only due to your ignorance about the Soul that you are embroiled in worrying about yourself alone. Banish your delusion! No matter who wins or loses, believe that it is you who shall lose and it is you alone who shall win. Else, as long as you consider yourself separate from others, you shall remain caught up in your desire to win as well as your fear to lose. And till then, you shall remain deluded and confused about this war and its outcome. Indeed, there is no remedy for such delusion!"

"Hence, know it for sure that the omnipresent Soul is the single source of life for everyone. Therefore, the thought of loss or win is, in any case, but an ignorance and a delusion of the human mind. Hence, in order to rid yourself of your present suffering, you shall have to sever the shackles of delusions that bind you such as winning-losing and virtue-sin at any cost. So, be brave and fight with all your might without worrying about the result. Leave the decision of winning-losing to Nature and its play. This is how a seeker of the Soul remains happy in each situation."

Krishna – The One and Only Complete Man!

Krishna is the only complete person
in the history of mankind.
Grasping the essence of
his life and his psychology
is the prime requisite
for people of the present modern age.

So far, I have elucidated a few verses of the Bhagavad Gita that describe the Soul. And I am sure, everyone must have got a glimpse of the Soul. However, if one is desirous of realising the ultimate height of the Soul, one has no option but to grasp the essence of Krishna's personality. One shall have to also understand why the wise savants consider Krishna as the one and only *Purna Avatar* or Complete Man. Of course, there are several reasons for it! In my book, 'I am Krishna'—a complete biography of Krishna—I have, at several instances explained in detail, the reasons why he has been called the Complete Man. Nevertheless, at present, we are discussing the Soul; thus, taking the Soul as a premise, let us understand why he is known as the Complete Man, as this shall prove helpful in comprehending the actual meaning of the Soul.

For this purpose, I shall have to quote a few verses of the Gita as reference. You may perhaps remember that at one instance in the Gita, Krishna says, "O Arjuna, as gems are strung together in a thread, so is this world strung in me." and "'I' alone am the cause of the creation and destruction of this world." He further enunciates that 'I' am the illuminator of everything, from the stars and moon to human life. Continuing in the same vein, Krishna says, "The power to give birth and rebirth based on one's *karma* is also vested in 'me'." While some ignorant people construe this as Krishna's ego, there are other ignoramuses whose belief leads them to worship Krishna in an idol form.

However, it would be prudent to dwell on the question as to why is Krishna repeatedly claiming himself to be the ultimate authority in this world. Is he deluded, is he an egoist or is he actually the ultimate authority in the world? So, in this context, you need to understand that Krishna was so rooted in the Soul that he was not even aware that he had a physical form that was addressed by others as Krishna. And when he is so unified with the Soul, it is but natural for the 'Soul' to talk with such authority. For, the Soul holds sway over all the occurrences; from the birth and death of human beings to the origin and destruction of the world. Everything occurs only because of the Soul. And when Krishna is nothing but a state of pure self-realisation, then he is bound to proclaim – 'I am the God of all Gods!' However, do remember, this experience of being the 'God of all Gods' is nothing but an absolute self-realisation of Krishna's Soul, and not of his body. And as no one other than Krishna has ever experienced self-realisation in its totality, no one has ever been able to proclaim renunciation with such authority and vivacity. While the others did manage to awaken the witness in themselves, they could not anchor themselves in the state of being a 'witness' in its totality. That is why, wise savants have called Krishna the one and only complete human being.

It is imperative to comprehend all this because people either idolise Krishna or they construe him an egoist and disregard him. However, both these categories of people are delusional about Krishna, because Krishna is just a pure Soul. Once you have comprehended this, try to grasp one more truth stated by Krishna. In the Gita, Krishna says, "O Arjuna, I am the Soul dwelling in the hearts of all, which does not differentiate between mine-yours. That is to say, the question of my Soul being greater or your Soul being inferior does not arise at all. The same Soul pervades equally in all human beings. And when the same Soul dwells in all, then the closest to us is our own Soul." Hence, you must bear in mind that it is nothing but ignorance to call out to the Soul of Krishna at the smallest instance. In the end, this too shall act as an impediment in your path of realisation of the Soul.

Well, I am sure everyone remembers that Arjuna too, was caught in a similar dilemma. He, too was unable to digest the 'tall claims' made by Krishna. Krishna says, "O Arjuna, it is but natural for you to doubt all that I claim because I am making these claims for the Soul and from the Soul, while you think I am referring to your friend 'Krishna'." Taking this explanation further, Krishna says, "O Arjuna, till you do not realise the Soul within, you shall not be able to comprehend the powers of my Soul-form. Hence, first recognise your Soul. Only then will you be able to recognise me."

Indeed, there is a lot to be grasped from this law enunciated by Krishna. Krishna's language is scientific and he speaks in terms of laws. And the term law implies that it is immutable; it cannot be broken. So, understand the intrinsic meaning of Krishna's words; Krishna is saying, "No human being can understand someone who is at a level higher than him." Hence, Krishna says, "O Arjuna, till the time you do not realise yourself in the form of Soul, you will not be able to recognise my form as the Supreme Soul." This is the reason why an ordinary human always remains deluded with regard to the actions of great people. This is the reason why the complete life of any great person is never discussed, be it Krishna,

Buddha, Christ or Socrates. As a matter of fact, everyone claims to believe in Krishna or follow him, but there is hardly anyone who knows even ten per cent about his life. The same is the case with Buddha, Christ and other enlightened Souls.

Nevertheless, in my book, 'I am Krishna' where I have presented the entire life of Krishna in the form of an autobiography, I have neither hidden anything about him, nor did I feel the need to do so. However, it becomes important to cogitate why several important aspects of the lives of great people are hidden or kept under wraps. The reason is clear! It is simply because the actions of great people are beyond the comprehension of an ordinary human being. They indulge in several actions which are unacceptable as per general beliefs and societal norms. Hence, those whose businesses thrive by propounding falsehoods in the name of these enlightened seers, fear that once the veil is lifted off the real incidents of their lives, they will lose credence of the people; and if this happens, it would spell doom for their organised business. Therefore, they stoop to manoeuvring facts by weaving fictitious and magical incidents into the life stories of these great people. But of what use are such stories that are far removed from reality? Yet, such practices are prevalent because the creators of such myths are neither able to understand, nor do they wish to understand the actual minds and lives of beings such as Buddha, Krishna and Christ.

In fact, with an aim to shatter this hypocrisy, Krishna states in the Gita, "O Arjuna, you shall experience the divine play and powers of this great Soul first in yourself and then in me. Unless you experience the Soul within yourself, it will be well-nigh impossible for you to comprehend me." And it is imperative to understand this point because people do endeavour to know and understand Krishna; some even make lofty, but useless claims. Alas! They remain caught up in the vortex of their own imaginary notions of Krishna. For, it is an indefatigable law that a human being cannot understand a person who is at a level higher than him. In other words, if one were to grasp Krishna in the truest sense, one has no option but to rise up to the level of Krishna.

In essence, only those who have elevated themselves to be anchored in the Soul will be able to understand the true personality of the likes of Krishna or any other great being. That is why, at one instance in the Gita, Krishna says, "O Arjuna—my devotee, my worshipper, seek my refuge and you shall be emancipated." Here again, mind well, when Krishna says 'my', he is not referring to his physical form as 'Krishna'; he is referring to the Soul. And whose Soul is he referring to? Not of Krishna's, but the Soul that dwells in all of us. So, let those running businesses of religion continue with their practice of propagating idolism of Krishna to fool people, but you should focus only on moving closer to your Soul. Thereupon, one day, you will be able to realise Krishna in the form of the Supreme Soul. And this is the message of Krishna for every human being. Hence, instead of wandering about in several directions, simply focus on attaining self-realisation. Know it with certainty that everyone is bestowed with the intelligence Krishna is discussing here. Hence, be kind enough not to squander this opportunity of recognising and realising the true form of the Soul.

Scientific Secret of the Soul

Whether it is human life or the universe, everything here transpires according to set laws... In other words, Nature's laws are basically, a formula, after understanding which there is no need to do anything. Adopt this formula and achieve anything you want.

So far, you have been privy to various introductions of the Soul. With the help of a few verses from the Bhagavad Gita, we have also reflected upon several facts about the Soul. Also, a comprehension is achieved for the fact that the Soul is omnipresent and reigns supreme, both within and outside. And that, this Soul is verily the ultimate authority in this world. After the discussions on the Soul so far, you must have grasped that as a human being is closest to his own Soul, in order to naturally experience its sublime powers and influences, a human being has no other option but to establish a close connection with his own Soul. And, this is the most important message of the Bhagavad Gita. Here, Krishna is not advising you to aimlessly wander in pursuit of establishing a connection with the Soul. He is neither suggesting worship or reading of scriptures, nor the practice of any Tantras or the chanting of Mantras. He is simply saying, "O Arjuna, within you resides the supreme power of this world in the form of the Soul. Instead of asking me, seek refuge in your Soul. For, your Soul is omniscient and knows everything that I know." Krishna is able to state this truth fearlessly, because he, unlike others has no business interests. That is why, he has not played upon your greed and fear. On the contrary, he is granting dignity to you. He is stating that the Supreme Power of the world dwells within you. Now, despite being aware of these facts about the Soul, if one still pursues to traverse on the path of ignorance and wander aimlessly, then the decision rests with him.

Nonetheless, you need to understand that the entire functioning of Nature, in spite of being mysterious, is bound by laws. However, psychologically, the common man has not yet evolved enough to be able to fathom the secret forces of Nature or experience them. But at least you must understand that when everything is bound by laws, it is but a Science. And the term 'Science' itself implies that it is possible to not only comprehend these secret forces, but also benefit from them by experimenting on them time and again. And as all these secret forces are a Science, they can well be understood and explained in scientific terms. Not just this, they can also be proved by experiencing them in the depths of the mind.

Consider this: Now, we all know the law that water evaporates at 100 degree Celsius. The point to note here is, even when Science was unaware of this law, water still evaporated at 100 degree Celsius. Similarly, the entire human life is bound by laws. It does not matter whether one is aware of this fact or not. Everything in human life is occurring in accordance with these laws. Hence, taking the analogy of conversion of water to steam at 100 degree Celsius ahead, the second point to comprehend here is, the definite occurrence of this phenomenon irrespective of the place and time, since it is a law. And just like the visible (e.g. water), all the invisible is also bound by laws. This means, in accordance with this law, the intensity of one's reaction at any given point of time is determined by one's state of mind at that particular moment. However, at present, we are not discussing the laws of the mind and its secrets; presently, our main focus is on the Soul. And in this regard, let me clarify that the Soul, too, is a part of this Science. Hence, not only can it be comprehended on a scientific basis, but it can also be experienced within. However, being invisible, it cannot be proved in any scientific laboratory, but it can certainly be experienced in the depths of the mind.

Hence, now we shall commence our discussion about the Soul in a scientific manner. As it is obvious that in this scientific age, a human shall be able to benefit from these secret forces only when these are discussed in a scientific manner. If you are totally receptive and allow these elucidations to directly enter the depths of your mind, I promise you that going forward, all your queries related to the Soul shall come to rest. Certainly, it shall then become very easy for you to experience the power of your Soul. This shall also help you to identify your weaknesses that prove to be obstacles on your path to the realisation of the Soul. Once identified, it won't take long for you to reach your destination. I hope, you are fully prepared to understand and experience the Soul in the laboratory of your mind in a scientific manner.

The Inner System of a Human Being

When the internal conflicts between your Mind, Brain, Ego, Senses and DNA-Genes will end, all the external conflicts will automatically end.

To comprehend the Soul in a scientific manner, first, a human being must have knowledge about his inner system. Surprisingly, though everyone is living, very few are aware of themselves or their inner system. For example, everyone is driving a car, but they lack knowledge about its parts such as the brakes, the accelerator or the steering. Under such circumstances, what would you expect if not daily accidents? Hence, the primary focus of every individual should be to fathom what lies within. It becomes mandatory for everyone to be aware of the powers that influence them within. How can one even think of transforming or changing their life for the better without an in-depth understanding of this? Ironically, everyone is engaged in attempting to comprehend everything else, except this basic truth. In such a scenario, how can one be expected to even steer one's vehicle of life in the right direction and arrive at one's destination, safe and sound? This, indeed, is the prime reason why everyone falters, and is unable to reach their goal! So, understand very clearly that whatever be the sorry state of one's life, it is so because of unawareness about oneself. In a nutshell, anyone who wants to drive the vehicle of his life smoothly, has to first comprehend his own system. In fact, the day when the children of this world would be educated about their inner system right from their early years, believe me, all the sufferings shall vanish from the face of this earth!

Hence, let us directly move forward to comprehending the inner system of a human being in brief. If you wish to comprehend all the inner powers that dwell within a human in a detailed and scientific manner, and if you wish to experience them and channelise them in the right direction, then you will have to read my book '*I am The Mind*'. At present, I am stating in brief what you must know in order to comprehend the Soul.

Without comprehending his system, a human being can neither attain happiness and success, nor joy and peace!

Everyone is aware that human life is affected by external factors such as circumstances. But very few know that way more than external factors, it is the inner powers that affect human life. In fact, all the outcomes in life are being determined by these inner powers. And the inner powers which affect human life comprise the mind, the brain, the senses and the ego. Besides, the deep impact of DNA and Genes is also evident on human life. And then, there is the Soul which is rooted in each human being with absolute firmness.

In short, these six forces are the inner powers of the human body which govern one's life. And everyone should at least

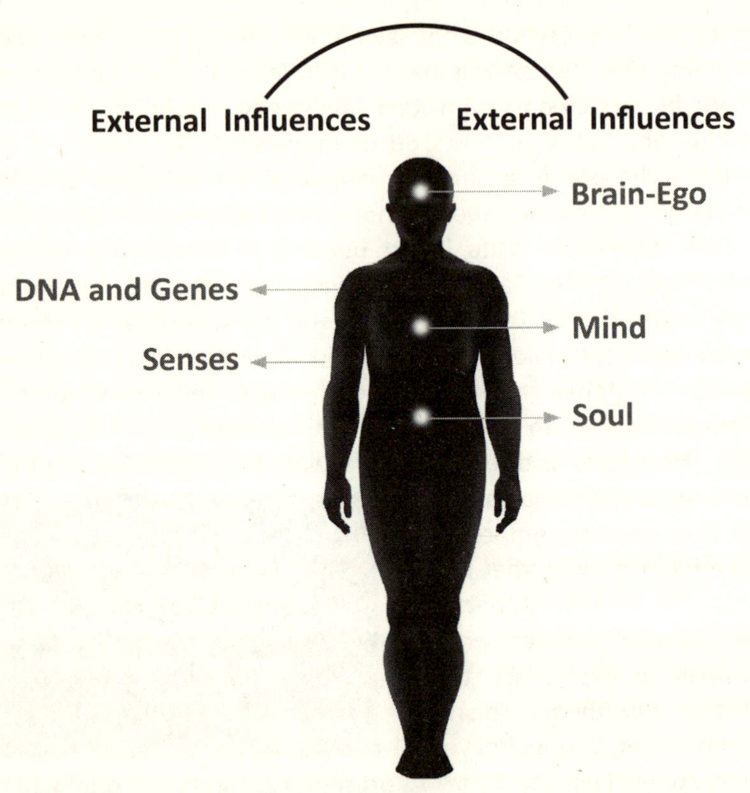

The Structure of A Human Being

It is a commonly held notion that human life is influenced by external circumstances. But far more than that, human life is greatly influenced by inner powers such as mind, brain, senses and ego. Besides, the deep impact of human Genes and DNA is also evident on human life.

be aware of this much regarding oneself. Here, one should also remember that the human is most affected by his mind. And a human being has not one, but seven minds. Here, you also need to understand that the ultimate mind, which is situated in the navel, is the 'Soul'. While some believe the Soul to be an intrinsic part of the mind, others consider it an individual entity by itself, separate from the mind. In any case, these varied viewpoints do not really matter much; as, the fact is, the Soul is not a part of the mind. The Soul, actually, is a state of 'no-mind'. In other words, the Soul is a state of void—nothingness. But in order to grasp the Soul in a scientific manner, it would be apt to consider the Soul as the seventh mind. Hence, be kind enough to not get into the argument of whether or not the Soul is a part of the mind, and thus, miss out on this opportunity of experiencing the Soul.

As many humans that many lives

As all the inner powers that govern a human's life are individual and different, every human being's life is different. If there is anything that is equally present in all, it is the Soul. Moreover, the course that a human being's life takes or will take is determined by the collective and mutual effects of the rest of the powers. Hence, in order to give the right direction to one's life, it is imperative for one to comprehend the functioning of all the inner powers that affect oneself. But there exist very few people who recognise and can distinguish between the inner powers that affect them, and their effects. And only the one who is able to distinguish between these two i.e. one's inner powers and their effects, can be considered to be living in awareness, while the rest of the people can be considered living in an unaware state! Needless to say, the unaware multitude, no matter how much they try, cannot carve a great life for themselves.

The flux of life from within

Surprisingly, to build a great life, everyone focusses on the outside world, whereas the truth is, life flows forth from within. And it is the inner powers of a human being that determine the state and direction of one's life. All the external manifestations, be it objects, people, events or anything for that matter which a human being considers as his life are nothing but a reflection of his inner self. First, events occur in the inner self of a person, and then they manifest in the outside world. This is the law of 'Time and Space' particularly with reference to human life and it is extremely important for everyone to grasp this well. This is because no one accords enough importance to what lies within, despite the fact that the entire life stems forth from within and just manifests in the outside world.

Until you change your Mind within, nothing will change on the outside. Because everyone is engaged in effectuating a change on the outside, no one is able to change anything at all.

Everyone has to realise that the roots of the problems that manifest on the outside, well lie within us. And till the roots are not treated, the external problems will not end. In other words, without first understanding one's inner self—what lies within—a person cannot free himself of a problem. That is why, in spite of incessant efforts by humanity in the external world, man is still mired in endless problems.

External life is just *Maya*—an illusion!

The entire external life of a human being is nothing but *Maya* or an illusion. This is because external life is not what life is all about but just a reflection of what lies within. Unfortunately, the human being, deluded by the perception of his brain and his senses, begins to perceive the outer life as real and lives under its influence day and night. And in this state of utter delusion, he presumes that all his problems too exist in the external world. Whereas in reality,

The Flux of Life from Within

All the external manifestations
which a human being perceives as his life
is nothing but a reflection of his inner self.
At first, events occur in the inner self of a person,
and subsequently they manifest
in the outside world.

that is not the case. Life and its problems both exist within. This is the reason, in spite of all his efforts, a human is neither able to gain anything nor is he able to find a concrete solution to end his problems. As long as a man perceives his outer life as his real life, problems will continue to envelop him. This is because, deluded by such fallacious belief, he will try to find solutions to all his problems in the outside world. Hence, everyone needs to understand that the outer life is just a reflection of one's inner self. Thus, no matter how much you experiment with your external life, it will not make an iota of difference. Get this straight—if you wish to change the reflection, you will have to change the form, which in this case is your inner self. As soon as the inner self is transformed, the reflection too shall change automatically.

Anything you see on the outside is nothing but a reflection of your Mind. Therefore, if you wish to solve the problems of your life, know well that the 'cure' lies in your Mind.

Thus, it is best for everyone to focus on improvement of the inner form rather than toiling and struggling in the external world to change the form. This is because external efforts do not bring about any significant positive result until they are supported by inner powers, as the roots of most events occurring outside lie within. Circumstances will improve in the outside world only when the roots within are treated. Nothing will change on the outside by mere wishful thinking for things to happen or not happen. Nor will taking recourse to external remedies have any significant effect on the transpiring events. Why don't you get this straight: the seeds that have germinated within will surely grow to become trees in the outside world!

In essence, I shall once again emphatically state that unless you become aware of your inner self, nothing will change for you in the external world. That is the reason, although everyone desires to change their lives in many ways, they are not able to do so. This is

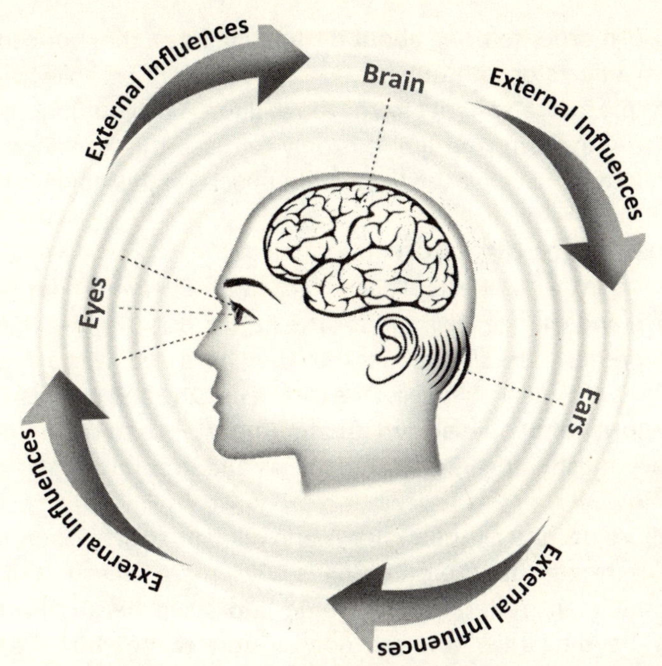

External Life is *Maya* – An Illusion

The entire external life of a human being is nothing but *Maya* or illusion. External life is not what life is all about, but just a reflection of what lies within. However, the human being, deluded by the perception of his brain and his senses, unfortunately, begins to perceive the external life as real, and reels under its influence day and night.

because in order to bring about desired changes, they concentrate all their efforts on the outside. I hope you shall be able to grasp this simple fact, and henceforth, you will focus on your inner self in order to transform your life. It is only to make this transformation possible that I have placed utmost emphasis on this point.

Take the right direction

It is a well-established fact that everyone desires to improve and change their life for the better. But they are not able to comprehend the simple fact that they have two lives as per the principles of Time and Space. One on the outside and one inside! As the majority of people accord greater importance to the outer life, they are mostly engaged in enhancing and grooming their outer lives. However, as this process in itself is wrong, they face nothing but failure despite all their talents and diligent efforts. Therefore, I would reiterate that the outer life is but a mere reflection of your inner self. I am reiterating this time and again because without comprehending this, you will not be able to head in the right direction. Hence, always remember that the one who wishes to enhance his outer life and attain great heights shall have to first transform his inner self accordingly. And in order to transform one's inner self, it is important to first understand what lies within. It is imperative to recognise and understand the effects of its various inner powers. In essence, you must realise that human life can only be transformed by grasping the functioning of all inner powers that affect a human and by bringing about a positive change in them. So, now we shall directly begin to discuss in sequence, the inner powers that influence a human being and their effects.

Effect of DNA and Genes

Primarily, the first power to affect humans is DNA and Genes. Thanks to scientific progress, today, we all know that a human inherits DNA and Genes from his parents. And as these are inherited from parents, often parental influence is evident,

DNA and Genes

Primarily, the first power to affect human life is DNA and Genes. Thanks to scientific progress, today, we are all aware that a human inherits DNA and Genes from his parents. And as these are inherited from parents, parental influence is quite evident on one's life.

especially in skin colour, physical structure, facial features, etc. At times, even certain habits are noticeable which starkly resemble those of one's parents and ancestors. Besides, the DNA and Genes play a domineering role in determining the physical health of a human being. It would, therefore, be prudent for everyone to comprehend the effects of one's DNA and Genes in depth.

The Functioning of the Mind

The human mind is a hurricane of idiocies and also the centre of many powers. Most importantly, the human mind is many births old. In other words, past lives have a much deeper influence on an individual's mind than his present life. And indeed, it is the mind which actually holds the reins of human life. Hence, it is the mind which determines whether one's life will be transformed or destroyed. That is why, it is said that a human being is nothing but the mind. But unfortunately, very few people know or understand the mind. In fact, very few people are cognizant of the fact that a human being has seven minds, including the Soul. However, in order to transform one's life, the human being shall have to comprehend his three chaotic minds and their functioning, and also the use of his three powerful minds. In fact, the first duty of a human being towards himself is to weaken his chaotic minds and activate his powerful minds. And to this effect, you must read my book *'I am The Mind'* as it shall help you comprehend the weaknesses as well as the strengths and powers of your mind. And as for the Soul, in this book, we are well discussing its effects in brief.

Presently, it would suffice for you to know that your entire life is governed by the mind. So, the more importance you accord to the comprehension of the mind, the more your life shall prosper. Because, the mind alone is responsible for the good and bad effects on your life. Based on this fact, you can well fathom the significance of the mind in your life. And when the mind is so significant, one shall surely have to comprehend it, right?! And as I mentioned earlier, the human mind has been in existence since

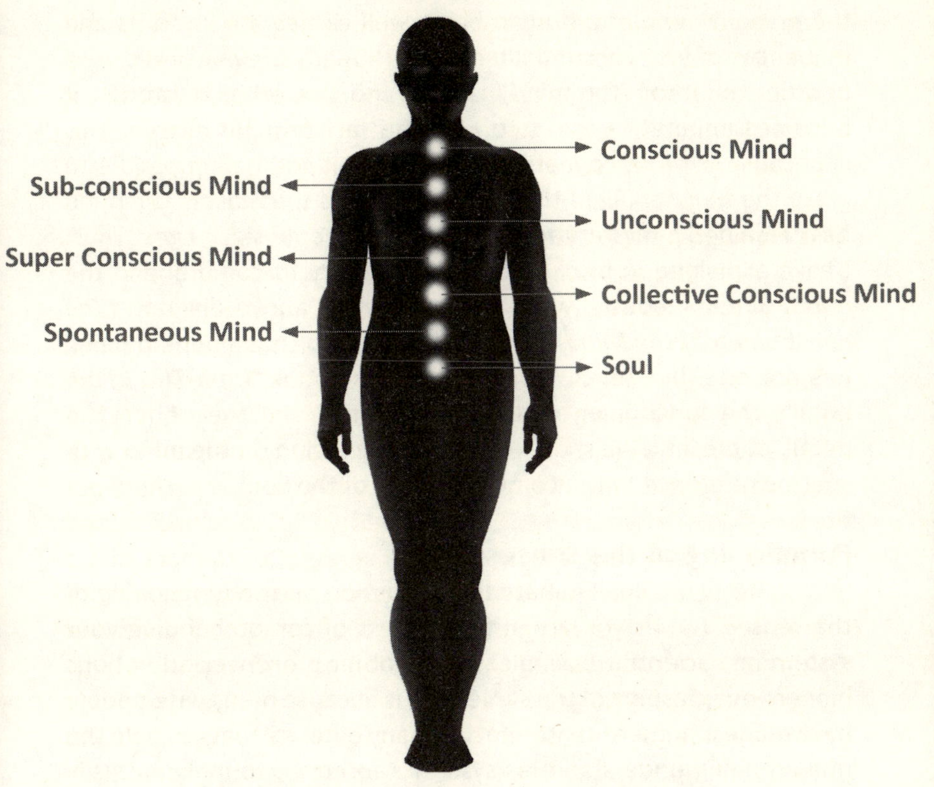

The Functioning of the Mind

The reins of human life are actually
in the hands of the Mind,
as the success and failure of life
is determined by the Mind.
Therefore, it is aptly said,
a human being is nothing but the Mind.

time immemorial through the evolution of many births. Thus, the present mind of a human being well carries the imprints and influences of vibes accumulated through many previous lives. And in order to fathom the mind in depth and unravel its mysteries, it becomes imperative for us to etch this fact in mind forever. This is because without cogitating on this fact, it will be impossible to grasp the functioning of the mind. And this is the reason, the mind has remained a mystery for a majority of people since ages. Thus, I have explained in brief all that is necessary to comprehend the mind. Simultaneously, with the help of the above diagram *(The Functioning of the Mind)*, you must also grasp that a human being has not one, but seven minds. And as my book *'I am The Mind'* entails the functioning of the seven minds and their effects in detail, at present, we shall restrict our discussion on the mind with specific reference to the comprehension of the Soul.

Functioning of the Senses

Now, we shall initiate the discussion on the functioning of the senses. But as you are in the process of comprehending your system in a scientific way, please do not let preconceived notions hinder your grasping of the same. This is because many wise people have made innumerous attempts in many different ways to help the human being understand his system. Moreover, to make it easily comprehensible, they all have used words and language specific to the era they lived in. Some have considered the senses to be a part of the mind, while others have recognised the senses as a separate entity from the mind. Some have referred to the powerful minds as the Soul, while others have labelled the powers of the mind as various *Chakras* (energy centres) and even Kundalini. So, if you wish to comprehend your inner powers in depth, you shall have to wipe out all your past learnings, and with a clean slate, allow this scientific method to seep into your mind. This shall soon enable you to experience all your inner powers. And ultimately, the aim is to recognise these powers, so it doesn't matter what names you give them. You must bear in mind that our focal point is to have an in-depth understanding of the powers, not their names.

So, without further ado, let us begin with the functioning of the senses. The senses of a human being namely the eyes, ears, nose, tongue and skin are the mediums that establish a man's connection with the outside world. The DNA and Genes have a deep influence over the senses. Besides, human mind also has a profound influence on the senses. And this effect of the mind on the senses continuously gives rise to the vibes of likes and dislikes in a human. All demands of human life, everything from taste to smell, have their roots in the senses. The vibrations of the physical and mental needs emanating from the senses also propel a human being to run endlessly in life. Here, it is imperative to note that along with the present birth, the past births also affect the senses in the same manner as they affect the mind.

Functioning of the Brain and Ego

Human brain and ego constitute a great force in themselves. The only difference is, unlike the mind, their existence does not date back to millions of years; both belong to the present birth. Attracted by the outside world, they both learn and imbibe many things with the passage of life which leads to their conditioning. Thereupon, they act according to their progressively formed conditioning. An important point to note here is, as both belong to the present birth, they are constantly in conflict with the mind which is in existence since time immemorial. Most of the time, both are at loggerheads with the mind. And here, it is important to understand clearly, that this conflict between the mind and brain-ego is the actual struggle that every human faces in life. Stuck in the conflict between these two, everyone is suffering as it is devouring all the life energy of a human being. Thus, it is imperative to understand this conflict between the mind and brain in depth. Without understanding the conflict between these two, it is impossible for anyone to understand much regarding their life. Until then, man will continue to wander aimlessly in circles, floundering, unable to comprehend which course he should take in life as well as the purport of his actions.

Honestly speaking, the conflict between the brain and the mind is responsible for all delusions and confusions faced by a human being. The brain desires to build a grand life with the help of external knowledge, while the mind desires to do so through its powers. And the human ego always acts in favour of the brain. The ego not only supports but also provides strength and firmness to the thoughts upheld by the brain. And as a result, the brain and the ego continue their two-pronged onslaught to suppress the mind, whereas the mind, which does not like to be suppressed, rebels against this suppression. This adds fuel to the fire of conflict between the two. Thus, from my end, I have explained in brief the reason for the ongoing conflict between the mind and the brain in every human being. And as this conflict prevails within you too, you must have surely grasped the crux of what I am trying to explain. If not, read the Bhagavad Gita carefully once again. For, in the Gita, Arjuna too was confused, caught in the conflict between his mind and his brain.

Why does the Mind not comply with your Brain and Ego? Simply because the Mind has been in existence since time immemorial, for innumerable births; it has experienced almost everything in existence. It is well familiar with the follies of the Brain and the Ego.

However, at present, all you need to grasp is, it is the conflict between the mind and the brain that is wreaking havoc in everyone's life. And in order to rise above this conflict, it is imperative for everyone to recognise the separate functions of the brain and mind. And then, it is also necessary to understand when, where and who should be your 'captain'. If you choose the wrong captain or pay heed to the wrong captain at the wrong time, you will never be able to accomplish your goals. In order to fathom the Soul, this bit of elucidation and understanding is sufficient. But yes, if you wish to comprehend the entire functioning of the mind and the brain, then you shall have to read my book '*I am The Mind*'. This book serves as the foundation for understanding the mind, life and mysteries of Nature, and that is why, I have to repeatedly mention this point in order for you to understand everything in detail.

First need of a human being: Understanding one's System

The first pre-requisite for a human being to lead a life to the best of his potential is to understand how his internal system functions and the effects it has on his life. Unfortunately, a majority of people are neither able to recognise the various parts of their system, nor are they aware of their distinct effects. Hence, everyone is seated in the driver's seat, holding on to the steering of their life, with scant knowledge of the system which will propel them forward in life. In order to aid a better grasp of this point, I shall elucidate the same with the analogy of a car. Firstly, in spite of sitting in the driver's seat, no one has an idea where the clutch, break and accelerator of their life are. If one drives recklessly thus, without proper knowledge on the expressway of life, what would you expect, if not an accident? And this is what is actually happening in the world. In life, man is encountering multiple accidents every day. Hence, bear it in mind that before embarking on the journey of self-realisation, the primary need of every human being is to thoroughly grasp one's own system, its composition and its effects. Therefore, please carefully imbibe what I am about to explain here onwards. If you find it difficult to understand, then carefully peruse it a couple of times till it is firmly lodged in your mind. But do not relent till you grasp the functioning of your inner system. Because only then will you be able to awaken the powers of your mind. And only when the powers of your mind are awakened will you be able to get a glimpse of your Soul.

Stop Wandering...!

Everyone feels that they are not getting
what they deserve as per their talent.
But it is not so.
For, in Nature, every moment,
justice is automatically being served.
Hence, find out the reasons
why you are faltering.
Only then will everything fall into place
and you shall progress.

In order to recognise your inner powers, let us take the analogy of a vehicle. Firstly, if one wishes to drive a vehicle, one needs to have a thorough knowledge about it. This knowledge is of utmost significance in order to drive the vehicle safely and smoothly. But in the case of a human, he is so 'brilliant' that he is trying to drive the vehicle without having all information about the vehicle. Similarly, all the teachings and education, whether they are being imparted in the name of religion and society or schools, colleges and universities, are engaged in teaching one to drive the vehicle of life without first understanding the composition of human system. This obviously gives rise to the question, how is this possible?! Well, all these teachings pertain to the outer realm, so let us forget them. They are bound to be deluding. But at least, a human being should be intelligent enough to realise by himself that without having the knowledge of his own system, he must not jump into the arena of life!

Hence, I beseech all of you to please be serious towards your life. And to this effect, the first and foremost step should be to try and comprehend your system. This is because without understanding your system, no 'knowledge' or 'effort' will prove helpful; even your talent shall fail you. As a matter of fact, even now, your talent has often been failing you. That is why dissatisfaction has crept in and everyone feels, they are not getting what they deserve according to their potential. However, they fail to comprehend the basic truth that it is not possible to make optimum use of one's potential without first understanding one's own system.

Therefore, let us now directly discuss the internal system of humans. And to that end, we have already comprehended the inner powers that affect a human being. We have also grasped that the state of one's life is nothing but the outcome of one's system. So, now we only need to understand the functioning of the human system. For, without understanding it, leading a glorious life is simply out of the question! Thus, if one wishes to improve one's life, then it is imperative to grasp one's inner powers as well as continuously fortify them. To transform life, no other solution will work except this. So, let us now discuss the role of a human being in conjunction with his inner powers, and how he can derive maximum benefit out of it.

Nothing can be done about the DNA and Genes

At the very outset, you must understand that you cannot do anything when it comes to DNA and Genes. You can neither change your facial features nor the complexion of your skin. Similarly, you

DNA And Genes Are Not In Your Control

You can neither change your facial features nor the complexion of your skin. Similarly, you cannot do much about your physical structure or your basic health as they are derived from your DNA and Genes.

cannot do much about your physical structure or your basic health. This is because all this has been derived from the DNA and Genes which you have inherited from your parents. However, with great strides made in modern science, it is now possible to obtain a report about the individual characteristics of one's DNA and Genes. Based on this modern scientific knowledge, it has become easier to mould our lifestyle, follow requisite exercise regimen and take preventive measures for good health. So, you must do all that is within your means and reach. But where you cannot do anything, you must accept it. Thus, I hope, it must now be clear to you as to how you must deal with your DNA and Genes; that is, what action you must take and what you should accept and move on. I don't think there is scope for any more confusion regarding this matter.

Let the senses function on their own

As we have already comprehended, the senses are affected by DNA and Genes and they also carry in themselves imprints of past births. Besides, they are also subject to habits developed in the present life. Even so, they function on their own. They exist in complete synchronisation with each other and function in perfect harmony. The human brain is the thread which keeps all the senses tied together. Hence, in order to keep the eyes, ears, nose, etc. functioning in the optimal manner, it is important to keep the brain fit and strong. Also, it is imperative to take proper care of all the senses, and in this regard, the comforts and luxuries provided by present-day science are extremely helpful. All that a human has to do with regard to his senses is to use them to the fullest advantage. As for the deeper effects of the senses, one must bear in mind that they have been impacted over several past lifetimes. Hence, instead of understanding or altering them, they should be left to themselves to function on their own. There is no dearth of teachings that encourage one to tamper with them, and you are attracted to such teachings as well! But I would still say, avoid interfering with the senses as much as possible. This is because no one has an idea about how much a human is suffering owing to these unnecessary interferences with the senses. Be it his health or his life, the human being is suffering its adverse consequences everywhere.

Therefore, everyone must realise that the human system has been created by Nature, and it is very powerful and potent in itself. Have faith in it, for it is most responsible. Every system is capable enough to bring about a positive change in itself. You should just leave the system to itself as much as you can and give it a chance to improve. Whenever you try to meddle with it, you will only make it worse. And then, you don't have to look too far; search in the life experiences you have had so far. You shall discover the truth by yourself. I understand, the habit of interfering with the senses is age-old and the pressure from the external world is also immense. Even so, try as much as you can to avoid unnecessary interference.

You are now living in a scientific age, and you all are sensible and intelligent. Then why do you pay heed to the outside world and interfere in the natural functioning of the senses? Think – When is your mind joyous? When it flows with the senses, or when it suppresses them? Then why do you unnecessarily suppress the poor senses? Why don't you understand that behind every vibration of the senses lie many hidden secrets? Hence, stop unnecessarily interfering with the senses at every instance without any plausible cause. Believe me, with this little insight, your mind and life shall soon be infused with a new, radiant joy!

Mind is on automation mode

As for the mind, it is imperative for everyone to grasp that the mind is completely on automation mode. At the same time, you must also remember, that the mind is under the influence of previous lifetimes spanning thousands of years. And that is why, it is bound to function according to the imprints gathered over all your past lives. The sudden vibrations that arise in your mind have their own hidden reasons and so is the case for the changes that take place in the mind. No teaching invented by a human can bring about a positive change in the mind. The fact that I have stated here is so significant that if you comprehend it, you will automatically realise the futility of the majority of teachings and knowledge. This is the reason why the majority of popular knowledge is contrariwise, distorting human mind. And this makes it imperative for everyone to grasp the complete science of the mind.

Nevertheless, for now, you must know that one's mind at present, irrespective of its state, is the culmination of the fruits of his *karmas* of past lives. And this is an extremely significant fact for everyone to comprehend. So, read this sentence over and over again and mull it over. For, this one sentence encapsulates many secrets of life. With the help of this one sentence, you must realise that talks of reaping the fruits of one's actions is nothing but extreme ignorance. Because, the result of each of your *karmas* is instantaneous and is immediately experienced in the form of your resultant state of mind. On the other hand, even to think of rebirth as non-existent or to think of it as fictitious is nothing but sheer ignorance. Therefore, know it with certainty that without absolute comprehension of the truth behind the fruits of *karma* and rebirth, one can never grasp any secret of mind and life. Therefore, my book on fruits of *karma* and birth-rebirth shall soon be released which will help people get a correct understanding of the subject. Along with it, you must also know that comprehending these facts with the use of the brain will not help much. Unless these facts seep into the depths of your mind in the form of 'an experience', no significant change will occur in your life. Hence, it is extremely necessary to delve into the mechanism of the mind and the secret forces of Nature, and take them seriously too.

Nevertheless, at present, you need to have an understanding of your mind; hence, moving further, let's delve deeper into the subject of the mind. It is an automatic instrument that functions round the clock. And the entire life of a human being is dependent on this automatic functioning of the mind. The automatic frequencies

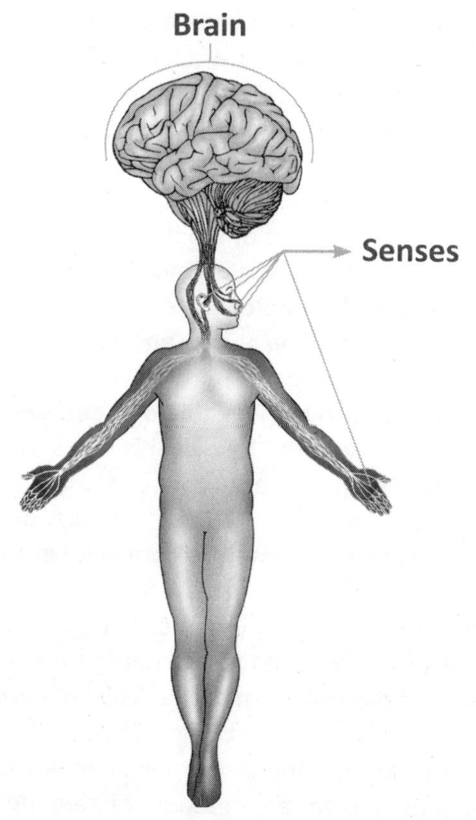

The Importance of the Brain

The brain is the thread that connects all the senses together. At the physical level, it is imperative to keep the brain strong if you wish to keep the eyes, ears, nose, etc. functioning well. At the same time, it is also essential to cater to the needs of all senses.

arising in the mind constitute human life and are also the source of his troubles. Therefore, the entire life is centered around this one knowledge—when should the mind be allowed to function of its own accord, when to interfere and how to improve its functioning. But unless this is grasped, it is better to allow the mind to function naturally. By interfering, you shall only end up corrupting the mind further. And here, everybody is hell-bent on interfering with the automatic functioning of the mind for no rhyme or reason. And caught in this vicious circle, a majority of people have distorted their minds. This is the reason the common man is now so perturbed by the chaotic tendencies of the mind. But believe me, it is you yourself, who has made the mind chaotic. Otherwise, the mind is a very beautiful and powerful instrument. Just do not tamper with it. At least wait till you have attained complete awareness and understanding of the mind. Till then, be kind enough to let the mind function as naturally as possible. Also remember, that in order to let the mind function naturally, there is nothing you need to do. If you stop interfering with it, it shall function naturally by itself. In other words, at the level of the mind, there is nothing you need to do in the initial phase.

The truth is, you have no option but to flow along with the automation of your Mind. Any interference or tampering will inevitably cost you dearly.

Brain-Ego – an independent power

So far, we have understood that along with parents, one's own past births also have a deep influence on DNA, Genes, senses and mind which affect humans. In other words, humans have no control over how these forces should be. Now whether or not they can be controlled, they are yours, howsoever they are. They surely have the effects and impressions of all your previous births' actions. Thus, whatever they are and howsoever they are, you can construe them as the fruit of your past births. And this is a profound secret that needs to be comprehended thoroughly, because it is for this very reason, that majority of their processes i.e. of DNA, Genes, senses and mind are automatic. In other words, now they are not in human control. Their reins are in the hands of other secret forces of Nature. Hence, now, no one needs to think or worry about their past lives or previous births' *karmas*. They are all a part of history now. As for now, 'today' or 'the present' is all one has and it is on the basis and support of 'the present' that one has to move forward and build a better future for oneself. Under no circumstances should one fall prey to the tactics and propaganda run by organised syndicates in the name of past lives and *karma*. And these facts pertain to you and you alone, and ideally, everyone should at least know this much about themselves.

In essence, a human cannot do much about the ongoing functioning of these three entities i.e. DNA-Genes, mind and senses. Yes, if he wishes, he sure can stop the processes of these three with the force of his brain and ego, and if he so wishes, he can manoeuvre them in a different direction. And this is the very supreme power of the human brain and ego which is constructive as well as destructive. Here, you must also comprehend that both the human brain and ego are the products of the current birth, that is, they are received and groomed in the present birth. Hence, whether it is the brain or the ego, without exception, both are almost absent in every child. But as he ages, with every effort that he makes in life and every piece of information he assimilates, the human brain and the ego gain in strength. In other words, a human being, through a medium of external influences, continues to condition these two.

To summarise, the mind, senses, DNA and Genes—the forces which affect the human being—howsoever they are, are present in the form of fruits of one's past lives. Hence, their reins are in the hands of Nature's system of justice. And based on this premise, the brain and ego are available to determine the actions one must undertake in the present life and the method to lead those actions to fruition. The human being enhances these two in this very present life and on their basis meddles with the mind-senses. This is the limited freedom endowed to human beings. And it is only in this regard, that everyone here is free. And one's life depends on how one exercises this freedom. It is certain that the one who suppresses the mind and senses on the basis of wrong teachings garnered by the brain-ego shall become perverse and frustrated. At the same time, one who wisely strikes a balance between them shall sail through. I hope, you all must have now gained clarity with regard to your inner powers.

Significance of comprehending the truth of rebirth

All secret forces of Nature are definitely profound, but they are not beyond comprehension as they are all law-bound. And as they are law-bound, they can well be proved in the laboratory of mind and life, and all my efforts are aimed towards the same. It is my conviction that without the fructification of the same, nothing can be gained. And it is not that these secret forces have never been discussed before. They have been discussed at length by many and have also been listened to with great zeal. A great amount of time has also been spent listening to these truths as well. But as they appear to be in contradiction with popular conventional beliefs, a human being is not able to repose his faith in them. In other words, more than lack of knowledge, there is lack of faith with regard to these secret forces. Needless to say, until a human being does not repose faith in them, how will he be able to implement them in his life? And unless he implements them, how will he be able to reap their benefits? And if he is not able to reap their benefits, he will be needlessly caught in an endless vicious struggle, facing the tempestuous blows of life.

I am stating these points so that you can focus on experiencing these secret forces in the laboratory of your mind that is, the workings of your mind. Once you give them a chance

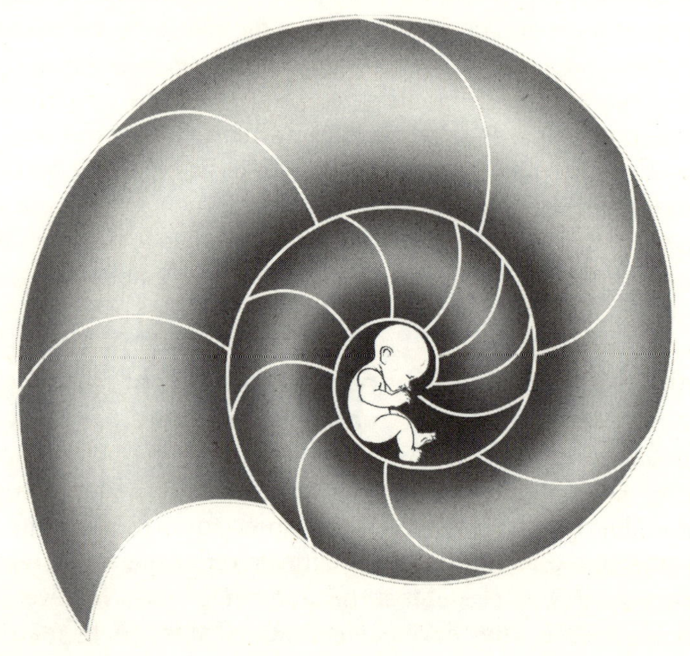

The Truth about Rebirth

It is true that a human takes many births. Whether it is your habits, your conduct or your talents, majority of them have no relation to what you have known, learnt or perceived in this birth. They are the fruits of your past birth *karmas* which have manifested themselves in the form of mind and senses in your present birth.

to be proven there, you shall also be able to implement them. And once you start implementing them, everything shall automatically begin to steer clear. Indeed, then it won't be long before you find your life transformed! So, now, without wasting any more time, let us directly try to grasp the truth behind rebirth. For, it is true that a human takes many births. And till a human does not realise this profound truth, he will not be able to easily comprehend any secret of Nature. In fact, it is due to his ignorance about this truth, that till today, a human is unaware of all secrets of life. I will obviously discuss about rebirth in detail in my book on rebirth. But, even in order to grasp the Soul, you will have to realise and experience this truth in your mind at least to some extent.

At present, even if not in detail, I shall surely have to explain to you in brief about rebirth, so as to enable you to understand the influence of the mind and the senses. And in this regard, you need to ponder, whether everything you have known, learnt or understood, has been known, learnt and understood in this very birth? Upon introspection, you shall find, whether it is your habits, your conduct or your talents, majority of them have no relation to what you have known, learnt or perceived in this birth. Then how and from where did they come to exist? Well, they are the fruits of your past birth *karmas* which have manifested themselves in the form of mind and senses in your present birth. Hence, you have no option but to grasp and accept the reality about rebirth. If you are wise, then a mere hint is enough for you. And if you have grasped the hint, you must recognise the difference between what you have known, learnt or perceived in this birth and that which belongs to your past births. As this clarity shall prove extremely useful in order to tread the path of life in sync with the secret forces.

Understand the mechanism of *Karma*

By now, you would have surely grasped your entire system and its functioning. If not, then read my explanation repeatedly but do not relent till you have grasped it thoroughly. Because without understanding it in totality, your life will not come in your control. Moreover, whatever is on automation anyway functions on its own. It is a common experience that whether it is the emotions of the mind or the desires of the senses, they ebb and flow of their own accord and reasons; they are not in anyone's control. However, the human brain and ego are not able to digest this because these two have garnered their own unique knowledge from the external sources. And this is the struggle of human life which no one is able to put an end to even after persistent efforts. Now, as you know, whatever is on automation is always active; no one needs to do anything to activate it. The mind and senses bear impressions of all past births, and they are self-governed, in sync with all the secret forces of Nature. And I have repeatedly stated that, this self-governed mechanism can also be called the fruits of *karmas* of all your past births. Hence, irrespective of the state of one's mind or that of senses, one has no reason to grieve or complain about them.

All in all, for now, you need to grasp that your mind and senses are fully connected to Nature's system of justice. If there is something not connected to Nature, then it is the human brain and ego. But a man has to traverse the journey of his life using the power of the brain and ego. In other words, those who wish to act now have no option but to work on their brain and ego, and move ahead with their help; the rest of your system is anyway functioning on automation mode. And as a matter of fact, it is at this juncture that the train of life is getting derailed. The plain and simple reason for this is, a human being is not able to take advantage of the positive aspects of brain and ego but he continues to suffer their negative consequences. And this, in itself, is the chief cause of human ruination. Hence, it is imperative to understand the negative and positive aspects of the brain and ego, in order to transform life and comprehend the Soul. Because till then, a human will not be able to grasp what actions should be left on automation and in which actions the brain and ego should be allowed to interfere. So, proceeding with the discussion, I shall throw light on this point.

Positive and negative aspects of Brain and Ego

So far, we have grasped that the human brain and ego have a very important role to play in the present life. Now, moving forward, you should also understand the chief roles the brain-ego play in your life. Firstly, it is only the human brain that can gain knowledge from external sources with reference to the current era. And one has no option but to live in accordance with the era one is born in. After all, we cannot think of travelling by chariots because our gods used to do so, for that will be nothing but sheer stupidity. That is why, to lead a life in sync with the present age, one shall have to learn to drive a modern-day vehicle and this task can be accomplished only with the help of the brain. In other words, to recognise the need of the prevalent time and era, and to learn to live accordingly, is the task of the brain. And this is the right use of the brain which one must make. At the same time, always remember that the human mind and senses have no relevance with the prevailing era, and this is where everyone gets trapped. For, while the mind and senses propel a human being to act under the influence of the impressions of past lives, the brain and the ego are bent on shaping his life in accordance with the present times. While the concern of the mind and senses is stretched over a series of births to happen in the future, the brain is concerned only about the present birth. Thus, the entire life of a human being is squandered in constantly battling the dilemma of 'who should he pay heed to'.

However, this is not the end of his woes. The problem with a human is that both his mind and brain are strong, independent and powerful forces. It is not easy to make either of them bend or surrender. Under the circumstances, it is obvious for the question to arise–Is it the brain that shall transform life or the mind? As both are powerful and useful, whom should one listen to? In this regard, I would like to make it clear that life can progress and prosper if the right balance is struck between the two. Even so, please make a note that in building your life, the mind's contribution is 90%

while that of the brain is just 10%. But as a majority of people are heavily reliant on the brain and ego, they are confused and their lives are ruined. From my end, I have given a clear indication to dispel this delusion and dilemma. We shall discuss it in detail later, when we discuss human structure, system and its functioning. For now, we shall confine our discussion to only what is required with reference to the comprehension of the Soul. In this regard, one must know that the human mind is a centre of communication to connect with the secret forces of Nature. And the human mind is an integral part of Nature's system of justice. Hence, there is a deep mystery behind every emotional upheaval that stems from it. This is the reason why the contribution of the mind in transforming life is much greater than that of the brain. But under the influence of wrong teachings and information, a human being passes the baton of the progress of his life to his brain-ego. And the brain and ego have a limitation that they can only comprehend man-made knowledge. They are completely oblivious to the secret forces of Nature, when in fact, life is highly dependent on the secret forces of Nature.

In a nutshell, you need to grasp that without nurturing your faith in the mind, you shall neither be able to inch closer to the Soul, nor shall you be able to transform your life. Thus, if you wish to make your life worthwhile, nurture your faith in the mind and use the brain only when required. Otherwise, you shall get trapped. This is the only plain and simple method to transform life. For now, I shall drop a few hints which will help you discern where you should use the brain and where you should not. Otherwise, to comprehend this in detail, you will have to wait for my forthcoming book on human structure, system and its functions. Unfortunately, as all secrets are interwoven with each other, it is not possible to explain all of them in detail at one go. At the same time, another compulsion is, in order to explain every secret, I have to inevitably hint at a few other secrets. I hope you can understand the difficulties I face while explaining these profound secrets to you.

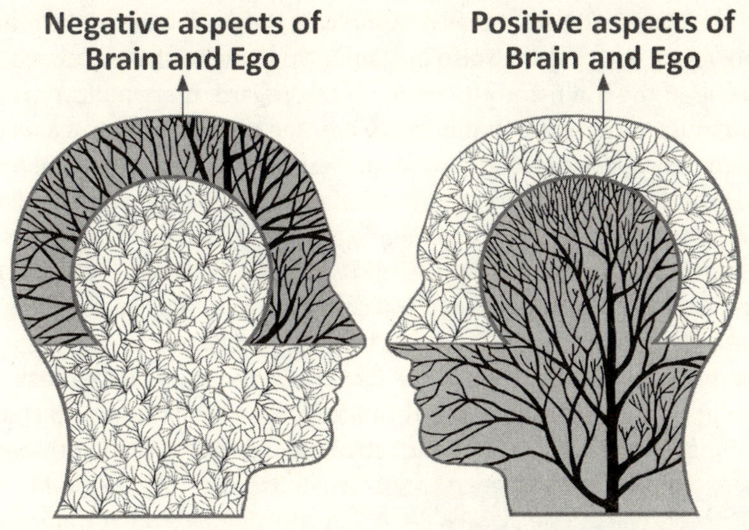

The Positives and Negatives of Brain and Ego

To recognise the need of the prevalent time and era, and to learn to live accordingly, is the task of the brain. Consequently, to identify the needs of life, make calculations and chalk out plans to this effect is also the task of the brain. And to provide firmness to these acts of the brain is the task of the ego. All in all, these are the assets of the brain and ego which everyone must use to the fullest. But to unnecessarily suppress the mind, senses and the physical body is the misuse of the brain and ego.

Nevertheless, I shall now indicate the usefulness of the brain too. Along with it, I shall also explain to you how to strike a harmony between the brain and the mind. In this regard, first and foremost, you must understand that in every era, the human mind has always been desirous of playing, frolicking, dancing and merry-making. And it is the brain that teaches one to play, frolic and dance according to the age one is living in. Similarly, the human senses have had a desire for exquisite fragrances and sumptuous delicacies in every age. But to fulfill these wishes according to the age one lives in is the task of the brain. Besides, it is the brain's function to understand the physical needs of the body for food. Similarly, it is the task of the brain to identify the needs of life, make calculations and chalk out plans to this effect. And the job of the ego is to provide firmness to these acts of the brain. All in all, there is no problem as far as these tasks are carried out by the brain and ego. But unfortunately, the human brain and ego do not stop here. They further get caught in the vicious circle of righteousness, good-bad and virtue-sin. They begin to make various mutual comparisons. And then, on the basis of their drawn comparisons, they begin to unnecessarily suppress the mind, senses and the physical body. They even start fighting against the effects of the DNA and Genes. It is due to these brash acts of the brain-ego that the human being gets mired in problems. And unfortunately, everyone construes this school of thought as the best knowledge, whereas in reality, this is nothing but sheer ignorance and foolhardiness. And on the basis of this ignorance, a human being is unnecessarily tampering with his mind, senses, body, DNA and Genes, which in turn, is making them corrupt and driving them away from Nature.

One cannot lead a happy and successful life without maintaining harmony between the mind and brain.

Now the question is–Why does the human being, driven by his ego and the strength of his brain, want to control the reins of his mind and senses that are in Nature's hands, especially when it is better to leave them free most of the time? The secret of human success lies hidden in the answer to this one question. However, I shall be able to discuss this in detail only while discussing about religion because, at present, we need to restrict our discussions only to that which is necessary for the understanding of the Soul. And in that context, it is imperative to know why the human being is unnecessarily tampering with his mind and senses, when actually such efforts are complicating his life further.

In order to understand why the human brain is unnecessarily tampering with the mind and senses, we shall have to understand the areas in which these three function. In this regard, one must know that likes and dislikes fall under the purview of the mind and senses. To decide whether these can be fulfilled or not is the task of the brain. And if the desires of the mind and senses can be fulfilled, then to decide the course of action for its fulfillment is again a task that falls under the brain's domain. But it is important for the brain and ego to be in sync with the mind and senses so that the laws of Nature are not breached while fulfilling those desires. We shall be able to discuss in detail which laws of Nature should never be broken in any situation, by any human being, when discussing the laws of Nature. Presently, you must grasp that the attempt of going against Nature to fulfil one's desires is proving to be disastrous. Else, I have already stated that the secret forces of Nature are so profound and interwoven with each other that they are surely comprehensible, but only one by one. So, you just start living in sync with one secret force, and then your mind will automatically establish harmony with the rest of the secret forces. The powers of your mind are fully tuned with Nature; they do not need any external knowledge. That is why, while elucidating the secret forces, I am also simultaneously trying to awaken the powers of your mind. Once they are awakened, you will no longer need to read these books.

Nevertheless, at present, you need to grasp that desires fall in the domain of the mind and senses. Labelling them as vice, bad or sin will digress you from your path of life. This is because the classifications of all virtues and sins are the products of human brain and ego. And it is humans who have given rise to ideas such as virtue-sin, good-bad, and not Nature. In fact, there is only one sin a man can possibly commit, and that is to go against Nature. So, remember forever, that without the right understanding, if the mind and senses are suppressed by the brain and ego on the basis of virtue-sin, good-bad, then they shall become perverted. And it has already happened with a majority of humans. This is the reason why everyone generally perceives the mind and senses as dangerous and chaotic. However, in reality, it is not so. This is just a punishment suffered by every human being for unnecessarily suppressing them. Hence, you must grasp the right uses of the brain, and thus save yourself from the repercussions of making inappropriate use of the brain. Only then shall the powers of the mind awaken, and only then shall Nature take the reins of your life into its hands. And only then shall life be transformed. I have now elucidated all that could be explained in brief regarding the inner powers that affect a human being such as DNA, Genes, brain-ego, mind and senses. But as this book is about the Soul, we shall now delve deeper into the realm of the Soul and comprehend its intricacies, which is necessary for us to inch closer to the Soul.

The Soul is Just a Witness

In every human being,
the Soul dwells in the form of
his 'Conscience' and 'Witness'.
As a proof, even though you may deceive others
when you lie or live in Untruth,
you yourself are keenly aware of your lie
and Untruth because of your Soul.

So far, we have discussed the inner powers of a human being, their influences and their functioning. However, there is yet another power which exists with all due firmness in every human being. And that is, his Soul. The Soul has been discussed since time immemorial and there are many theories and concepts framed around it. But what is the Soul? What is its role in human life? To find the answers to these questions, let's begin with understanding the fact that the Soul existent in a human being is a mere 'witness'.

And by 'witness' it is implied that the Soul is a mere spectator to the events occurring in a human's life. And when it is the spectator, it certainly has no role to play in the functioning of the entire human system. The entire play of human life revolves around one's mind and senses, and the brain and ego act as a fuel or deterrent in this play of the mind and senses. As mentioned earlier, the Soul has no interference in this play of life. It neither stops the brain and ego, nor does it propel the mind and the senses for anything. The human Soul is just a witness and remains a witness in all circumstances. It just watches both the inner play of the human system and the outer events that unfold as a result of this play. All in all, the entity that witnesses all that is happening inside and outside of a human being is called the 'Soul'.

You are the Soul

From all that we have discussed so far, it is now clear that two sets of powers are existent in a human being. One exists in the form of his mind, senses and brain-ego, and the other, in the form of his Soul. In other words, the first is the realm where everything is occurring, whereas the other is a mere spectator to the play of these powers. Now, it is obvious for the question to arise: 'Who are we?' Are we the 'doers' or are we the 'witness—the spectator'? In order to grasp this scientifically, you shall have to understand the practical functioning of your system. For example, when you see something, how does the realisation of what you see come about? Certainly, through your eyes it is transmitted to your brain. In other words, your brain becomes aware of what you see. This means, you are not the eyes, rather you are the brain; because in the end, you can only be the entity which becomes aware. So now, tell me, who is becoming aware of this thought process of the brain? Well, that which is becoming aware of it, is your Soul. Similarly, who becomes aware of an emotion arising in the mind or anything desired by the senses? Certainly, your brain! Then the brain decides what to do about the desire that has emerged in the mind. But then again, there is someone who is becoming aware of this play between the mind and brain! And that who is becoming aware is 'you'! That itself is your Soul. This, in turn, clearly implies that you are certainly not the eyes, ears, body, mind, brain and senses, because the doer and the witness cannot be the same. So, take your attention off the 'doer' and focus on the 'witness'. By constantly and repeatedly focussing on the witness, your spiritual awareness will grow. As awareness grows, you shall begin to realise that you are the one witnessing the play. So, just continue to let this experience of being a witness grow deep within. Your life shall automatically take a positive turn and start changing for the better. I am sure, with this elucidation you would have gained a clear insight into who you are and what the Soul is all about.

How to be anchored in the Soul?

Having grasped what the Soul is all about, now the next question is – How to be anchored in the Soul? And this question has confounded people for ages. History bears witness to the fact that none of the suggested paths has ever benefitted mankind. Whenever and whoever has attained self-realisation, it has been a sudden occurrence. Yet, those running organised business in this field have no qualms in suggesting the path that they deem fit. However, you must understand that the very question, 'how to be anchored in the Soul' is fundamentally wrong. Because, in truth, you are but a pure Soul. So, the very question—how to establish oneself in the Soul—is in itself fundamentally wrong. And, the premise of this question is verily the ignorance that prevails about the Soul. This ignorance prevails because instead of considering yourself as the Soul, you believe yourself to be the mind, brain, ego, body and the senses. Also, to the misfortune of human beings, the external teachings provided to them are based on the same (false) premise. But as these teachings are wrong and delusional in nature, they have been proven ineffective. This is because, as long as you consider yourself the mind, brain, ego, body and senses, you shall continue to tamper with them. And as long as you continue to meddle with them, you will inevitably be interfering with many things in the external world. And you must bear in mind that you cannot be anchored in the Soul by way of any kind of interference or tampering. I have revealed such a deep secret here that if grasped, most of the other teachings shall become irrelevant for you. Thus, for a better understanding, I would reiterate that the Soul, in all circumstances, is the 'witness' and not the 'doer'. In fact, being a 'Soul' well implies that the onus of all my actions lie with the secret forces of Nature; under all circumstances, I am just the spectator watching this play unfold. Therefore, you need to understand that each tampering, each interference shall surely drift you away, not only from your Soul, but also from the secret forces of Nature.

Honestly speaking, this is the point where all the paths and useless teachings become redundant. Because you are only a witness and a witness does not need to interfere. And if you interfere, then you no longer remain a witness. There is no middle path for self-realisation. No person can be anchored in the Soul unless he stops considering the system as his own. And unfortunately, the knowledge at your disposal, for one reason or another, teaches you some or the other form of interference. This is why, self-realisation, which should have been a commonplace occurrence, appears to be a rare phenomenon to human beings.

Well, from my end, I could not have been more explicit than this. I have already stated that you should not ask how to be anchored in the Soul. Don't make any efforts in this direction, else you shall go even more astray. If you really wish to be closer to your Soul, then you should weaken your delusion of considering yourself as the mind, brain, senses or the body on a daily basis. The more successful you are in weakening this delusion, the greater shall be your proximity to your Soul. Because your interference with any of these entities will automatically become lesser to that extent. Bear in mind, this is the only path to move closer to your Soul. And to this effect, you do not even have to make incessant efforts over the course of innumerable births. Remember, a wise man, if he so wishes, can, from this very moment become the witness to the play of his life.

Why is the human deluded about the Self?

Now, it is obvious for the question to arise – When a human being is a witness, why is he considering himself to be a body and its system? A plain and simple answer to this question would be, propelled by the brain and ego, the human comes under the influence of the external world, and under these influences, he charts out a list of his needs. And consequently, he engages himself in all kinds of futile exercises to fulfil those needs. In other words, ensnared by external attractions, he identifies himself with his 'system' instead of recognising himself as the 'Soul'. Ironically, it is the proliferation of wrong teachings in the world that misleads a man to tread the wrong path. Based on these teachings, he makes countless lists of dos and don'ts for himself such as good-bad and sin-virtue. And then on the basis of these lists, he begins to suppress his mind, senses and body. Eventually, caught in this vicious circle, the one who was meant to be a witness, becomes the doer. Thereupon, he not only creates chaotic situations for himself in the external world, but also lives in a constant state of turmoil internally. But this was, is and shall remain the path that leads one astray. As is the law that the more chaos one causes on the basis of the brain and ego, the more one goes astray. Because, how can you possibly interfere in a system or life that is not your own?! You just cannot! And to kindle this awareness is the only true knowledge. In fact, this knowledge is the only path that leads to human upliftment. In fact, interfering

Not only your possessions, relatives, friends and foes, but even your vacillating emotions are 'others' for you. You are merely a spectator, watching their play.

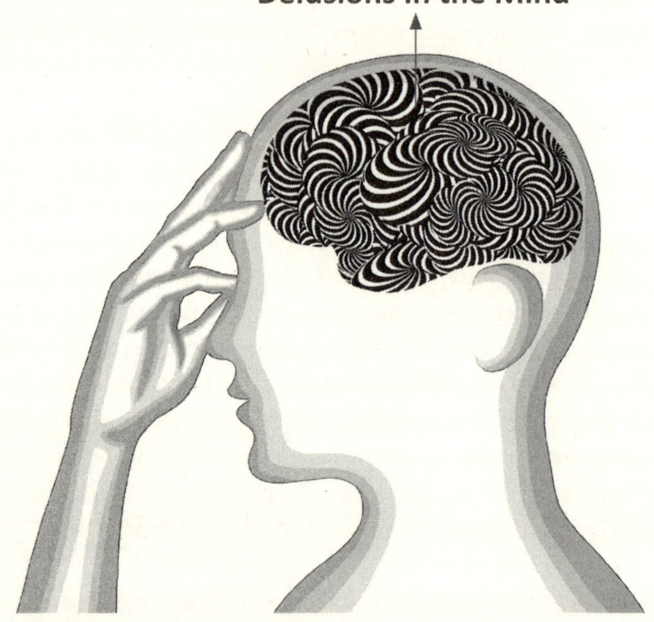

Why is a Human Being Delusional?

Lured by external influences,
a human being erroneously identifies himself
as his 'system' instead of the Soul.
But how can you interfere with a system
that does not belong to you?
It is a law that the more chaos one creates
due to their brain and ego,
the more delusional he becomes.

or tampering with one's system is the greatest form of violence. And today, a majority of people have fallen prey to this violence. Ironically, it is these very ignorant people who then vociferously preach non-violence!

If you decipher carefully, in the Gita, Arjuna was trying to indulge in this very form of violence. In spite of his mind being consumed by thoughts of war, being trapped in external influences, he was trying to evade them; and that is when Krishna had said, this very act of going against one's system is violence. As long as war or its thought exists in the mind, one must not run away from the war. If one's mind attains the awareness akin to that of Gautama Buddha, then it is a different matter. But swayed by the influence of ordinary scriptures, Arjuna is construing war as violence. Whereas, according to Krishna, to act against one's mind is violence. Indeed, what Krishna is enunciating is the only true knowledge; rest all knowledge doled out in the world is but a delusion! This is because how can you interfere with something that does not belong to you, which in this case, is the 'system'? This is the reason why the Bhagavad Gita is the ultimate knowledge, far removed from all useless beliefs. This is also the reason why the Bhagavad Gita is the only recourse for humans to attain spiritual awareness and self-realisation. Here, you must also clearly understand that without first becoming free of preconceived superficial knowledge or what you have heard or perceived, you cannot grasp the Bhagavad Gita or Krishna. And if not today, tomorrow you shall surely have to grasp the essence of Krishna. This is because without inching closer to your Soul, you shall reach nowhere in life and will never be able to taste success. This is the science of success for a human being. However, I shall be able to elucidate this science in depth only while discussing the science of religion. As for the present, I have explained many aspects of the Soul in great detail to rule out any scope for confusion. Hence, be determined and get closer to the 'witness', for then, believe me, it won't take long for your life to be transformed.

In a nutshell, true knowledge lies in knowing that this system is not your own. And supreme knowledge lies in the realisation that when the system does not belong to you, then you have no right to interfere with it. Once you have imbibed this knowledge in your life and adopted it as a way of life, you shall automatically be anchored in your Soul, become a 'witness' and attain wisdom. Now, on my part, I have endeavoured to explain everything that one could possibly explain in brief about the Soul in a scientific manner. This explanation is plain and simple as well as easy and practical. If you are facing difficulty in comprehending it, then it is your old habits coupled with futile, accumulated knowledge which is proving to be an impediment. If one were to get rid of these two, then for everyone, everything is readily available on a platter from Nature. Now, the choice is yours, whether to keep trudging in life in spite of making incessant efforts, or achieve the unsurmountable heights in life whilst living in a relaxed, peaceful state of mind! Because it is the law of life that one who gets closer to the Soul will progress, while the rest will just continue to trudge along and suffer the blows of life. Nothing will work for them - neither their beliefs or traditions, nor their futile knowledge. In fact, without the Soul, even their own talents will fail them.

Whether it is our arrival or departure from this world, or the functioning of our system, everything is automatic. Where is the scope for even the slightest interference in this?

System – Your Board of Directors

So far, you must have at least grasped, that you are a witness, absolutely different from your system, which you have assumed as your way of being. Now, you also need to understand that your system, in itself, is the Board of Directors; even so, it certainly does not belong to you. You are but a pure witness. So, the simple solution is to leave the system alone, and not meddle with it. When the system does not belong to you, why should you be bothered about it in the first place? Why do you not realise that you and your system are two different entities? Why do you needlessly believe that the problems of this system or the subsequent chaos caused by it are the problems of your life? Why do you not understand that when the system is not yours, then what do you stand to gain or lose? You just sit back and enjoy the show!

Therefore, all you need to do is, do not allow the brain-ego to take the wrong path. Control them with the help of your three powerful minds. Do not allow your brain-ego to come under external influences and unnecessarily overrule your mind and senses. Life belongs to the system, and not you; so let the system rule. Let the system on its own decide what actions are to be performed, when should they be performed and what their intensity or duration should be! You must not interfere with it. If there is a conflict or contradiction between the brain and the mind, then let them deal with it; why should you be concerned? With this one habit, your witness will continue to grow stronger.

You must comprehend it well that if you come under the influence of anything that unnecessarily suppresses the mind and senses, then let alone the Soul, you will not be able to enhance even the powers of the mind. Honestly speaking, man has lost the extremely potent powers of his mind as he is unnecessarily mired in the knowledge of what is good-bad. This is because if anything is good-bad, it is your system, which is not you. So, let the system worry about itself. Why are you losing your mind over it? But unfortunately, this has now become a habit with not just you but everyone, and that is why, everyone's life is mired in problems. However, if you wish to save yourself, then you must move determinedly towards your Soul. And that step is to reinforce this belief in yourself that 'When the system is not my own, why should I care about it? It is responsible for itself, so let the system worry about itself.' This is all you need to do; the rest will fall in place automatically.

Let the system function on its own

By now, you must have grasped that except for your brain and ego, your entire system is on automation, which means, you can neither generate anger or joy in your mind, nor can you decide the time when the body should fall asleep or when it should feel hungry. Neither can you decide when and what the senses would desire to eat. This entire process is automatic and it is in your best interest to leave it on automation as much as you can.

If you protect your brain-ego from the influence of wrong teachings; if they are not ensnared in the vicious circle of good-bad or sin-virtue, then they will allow your system to function on automation mode. Thereupon, when the body feels tired and sleepy, the brain will allow the body to rest unless there is an important task to accomplish. If the body feels hungry and the brain is not conditioned to fast on certain days, then it shall allow the body to eat. If the mind desires to play and there is no obstacle in it, then the brain-ego shall allow it to play. This is because, for a true witness, these are not his problems but that of the system. And when the problems are of the system and when everything at stake is also of the system, then let the system deal with it. Why should you meddle with it?

Trust me, with this one habit, you shall get closer to the secret forces of Nature. You are just the spectator, hence, try to remain the spectator as much as you can. Know for certain that with this habit, soon you shall become one with the supreme Nature. Then, to improvise the system and to accomplish great tasks through the system will be the responsibility of the secret forces of Nature. As ultimately, the system also belongs to Nature, not you. And if it does not belong to you, then the responsibility also does not rest with you. So then, why do you want to take the onus of something which is not your responsibility at all? Why indulge in a task that you are not capable of performing? Why do you not understand that with your efforts and interference you have reduced your system to this pathetic state! Now at least hand it over to Nature! It is Nature's responsibility; let Nature improvise it. You are here just to enjoy the show, so sit back, relax and enjoy it.

As you sow, so shall you reap

Yet another point to comprehend here is, for no rhyme or reason, you are being persuaded to indulge in or refrain from many actions from all corners. Ironically, you too are following them without having an inkling of the harmonious functioning between your system and the secret forces of Nature. Moreover, your failure in comprehending that your problem does not lie in 'doing', rather in suffering the consequence of that 'doing', intensifies your problems by leaps and bounds. Hence, you must understand that when you do nothing, you shall also not suffer the consequences for the same! Hence, let the system act, and let the system bear the consequences too! All you have to do, is watch the show that your system plays and the consequences it bears as a result. You just bear in mind that you have come here to enjoy life akin to the experience of watching a movie. So, sit back and enjoy the show! Once you have comprehended this profound truth, you will instantly be liberated and be able to enjoy life in its true sense. Because as soon as you understand that your problem is not in 'doing' but in bearing its consequence, then automatically your 'doing' shall reduce. And no sooner 'doing' reduces than you shall inch closer to the Soul, and become the spectator. And as soon as you become a spectator to the movie of your life, you shall immediately become a spectator to the films of others' lives as well. Imagine, how much you shall enjoy watching so many movies at the same time! Nevertheless, know for certain,

You are gripped by ego
when you have made an effort
to gain or achieve something.
But how can those,
who have received everything
automatically,
be suffused with ego,
even if they wish to be?

that you are here only to enjoy as a spectator. And as you are the witness, you were, you are and you shall always remain free. I have, on my part, endeavoured to reveal the easiest way to attain supreme freedom or emancipation. Now, it is up to you to benefit from it as much as you can.

Why is it important to get closer to the Soul?

So far, you must have at least grasped that there exists a system in us which is the 'doer', and there is a Soul that is the spectator to the show played by that system. The question is - Why should we get closer to the 'witness' than the 'doer'? What is the harm in living, considering oneself as the system? Well, the only harm is, one who considers himself to be the 'doer' shall surely 'do' a lot. And the truth is, whatever he will do shall only complicate his life further. So, think, when you do nothing, would your mind, brain and body become dormant? Will they remain inactive and do nothing? Of course, they will not remain inactive! Even when you do nothing, they will remain fully active. Now think - When you would be doing nothing yourself, who shall be driving your system? Well, the supreme powers of Nature! Thus, true knowledge lies in acknowledgement of the truth that this system belongs to the Supreme Existence and only the Supreme Existence should be operating it. We are here to just enjoy this play between the Supreme Nature and this system; this is the reality of human life. And one who wants to experience this enjoyment shall surely have to stop 'doing' everything.

Indeed, if 'doing nothing and simply enjoying the show' is the best way to live; then where is the problem? The problem is, all teachings imparted unto humans are inciting one to indulge in one action or another. In fact, many of your teachings are even prohibiting you from several actions! And caught in the vicious circle of these teachings, you are no longer able to comprehend that 'a lot can happen without doing anything'! Although, I will be able to have an in-depth discussion on 'how great things happen without really 'doing', only in my book on automation; for now, you should comprehend that if wise people are calling 'mere action' a sin, then they are not wrong. This is because 'doing' is a sin, irrespective of what you are 'doing'. Similarly, 'witnessing' is a virtue, irrespective of what you are 'witnessing'. The same wisdom has been imparted by Krishna to Arjuna in the Gita – "As I am the witness to the war, I will not incur sin irrespective of the enormity of violence in the war. On the other hand, as you are desirous of performing an action of deserting the battlefield as a 'doer', you shall be a sinner in any case." This is why Krishna is explaining to Arjuna – "If you consider the 'system' to be your own and run away from it, then it will lead to disaster. Instead, if you consider your 'system' to be just an instrument of the divine and surrender it to the Supreme Existence, then you shall be liberated, in spite of fighting the war."

Nevertheless, this book is not about the Bhagavad Gita. So, limiting our discussion on the Gita, you just need to understand that the secrets of life are plain and simple. The only truth is, the system does not belong to you, it belongs to the divine. Then whether it is good or bad, it is not the subject of your concern; it falls under the divine's domain of worry. And true religiousness lies in leaving worries of the system to Nature. You shall go completely astray if you believe the system to be flawed and consider any method of purifying the system as a virtue of religiousness. These are profound secrets of life! You just need to grasp the secrets I am revealing one after another, imbibe them and inculcate them as a way of life as much as possible. The rest shall fall in place on its own. For now, you just need to grasp, why should you be needlessly worried about a system that does not belong to you? Why should you interfere with that which is not yours? Once you realise this, you shall soon find happiness, joy, peace and love!

Everyone here is just a medium—an instrument of Nature

Let us now delve into the science of realising greatness. This is because, ultimately, everyone is living with the aim of becoming great. But as they become dependent on the brain-ego to this effect, they tend to miss out on attaining greatness. This is because the human brain and ego insist the mind and the body to be ever-ready to fulfil their desires and demands. Due to this insistence of the brain and ego, everyone here keeps straining and restraining their mind, body and senses. And for this very reason, one gets mired in innumerable problems. This is because to unnecessarily torture the mind, body and the senses simply means fighting against the secret forces of Nature. On the other hand, when the human being leaves his system to function on its own and becomes a mere witness, then Nature takes charge of his system. As a result, all the great powers of Nature utilise that individual's system for the greater good. In other words, Nature then makes him its instrument, a medium to execute its plans for the greater good. And this is the very reason why the system of that human marches towards accomplishing great tasks. This is the secret behind all great people achieving legendary success and becoming historic figures. And remember, the witness, that is you, at that time too, remains a mere witness to this play between Nature and the system. This is the reason why no great human being ever becomes arrogant about his accomplishments and historic feats. For, he is well aware that he did not play a major role in the great deeds accomplished through the system. The Supreme Existence made those accomplishments possible by using the system as an instrument. In that case, how can such a person claim, "I did it!"? Only those who are engaged in religious ritualism and whose system is driven by ego, are compelled to arrogantly proclaim, 'I have done it!' I have given you a hint, grasp it if you can!

Soul has a Direct Relation to Life

The Brain, the Ego, the physical body and the automation of the Mind differ from person to person. But, at the level of the Soul, there is no difference; all are 'One'.

How phenomenal is the play of Nature that even while doing nothing, the Soul is, in fact, the be-all and end-all for a human being! Although the Soul is a mere witness, a human cannot accomplish anything great in life without moving closer to the Soul. This is because Nature has sole control over everything great in existence and this greatness from Nature flows forth only through the system which has surrendered itself to Nature; and this surrender is not possible without becoming the 'witness'. Hence, the one who wants to become big and great in life has no option but to become a witness. In other words, he has no choice but to get close to the Soul. And getting close to the Soul is the only true religiousness. That is why, it is said that without achieving spiritual success, no worldly success can be attained. Although I shall be able to discuss this entire science in detail in my book based on Dharma-religion; at present, just let this fact sink into your mind that without getting close to your Soul, you cannot become great in life.

One Soul - Many Systems

With regards to the Soul, there is yet another point which needs to be comprehended thoroughly; and that is, there is only one Soul in existence and that Soul alone is the pure witness. If there is anything different in everyone, it is the mind, brain, ego, body, senses and the DNA and Genes. This is the reason why in spite of being a 'pure witness', Krishna, Buddha, Christ, Kabir, Meera, Lao Tzu and Ashtavakra are all different from each other. Don't ever presume that in order to become the witness or to realise the Soul, you shall have to cease the functioning of the mind, brain or ego; only the ignorant speak thus. All these entities are inseparable parts of our body and existence. And, as long as the Soul dwells in the body, they all will remain present and active too. The only difference is, as soon as one becomes a 'witness', they all elevate to be in sync with Nature, and automatically begin to function like Nature. For day-to-day functioning of life, as long as one is alive, an individual will naturally continue to feel the pangs of hunger and feel the need to rest. I am explicitly stating this because a lot of delusory information regarding the witness is popular among the people, when in fact, being a witness is a very ordinary process. It is a false belief that upon becoming a witness, the mind, brain and ego cease to exist. On the contrary, the truth is, a witness no longer considers them as his own.

Hence, do not fall prey to these meaningless talks and digress from the path of life. All these talks unnecessarily trigger feelings of inferiority and sinfulness in humans which mislead people into narrow, parochial lanes of sects, communities and organisations. However, this is a web of illusions, so do not be ensnared in it. Instead, trust me and move forward with the faith that the journey of being a witness is not at all arduous or long. You are a witness and being a witness is the only reality of your existence. Moreover, being established in one's reality cannot be a Herculean task, can it? So, if you let this ordinary occurrence remain ordinary, you shall soon be anchored in your being. But if you make it complicated or arduous, you shall continue to wander until you lose your way.

A human is prey to wrong teachings

The sole reason why a human finds himself in such a despondent and unsuccessful state today, is because he is attracted to wrong teachings. The only teaching a human being needs to imbibe is — he is a 'witness', this alone is the reality, and this alone is the truth. And when he is a witness, he must not interfere with his system. There exist many profound secrets and many great laws of Nature behind this. But as a human being is ignorant about these secrets and laws, he is being bombarded with teachings from all around on how to tamper with his system. In this process, the 'witness' in a human is becoming weak and the 'doer' is growing stronger. But this doership is the only ignorance as well as irreligiousness. Hence, without first shielding oneself from the influences of these wrong teachings, no one shall be able to bridge the gap between himself and the Soul. On the contrary, the growing sense of doership and his act of suppressing the system, widens the chasm between him and the Soul, resulting in his mind becoming increasingly distorted; and this, unfortunately has already happened with the majority of human beings. So, remember, you were a witness, are a witness and shall always remain a witness. Keep dwelling on this truth day and night; this is the only way to your emancipation.

Saint Ram Travels to America

You are not the doer of the action,
nor the one experiencing it.
You are just a witness.
So, sit back and just enjoy the show!

In order to facilitate a better comprehension of the Soul, let me narrate an interesting story. Long ago, there lived a saint named Ram in India. Once, he visited America at the request of his disciples. The saint had a peculiar mannerism of dressing which often drew looks of amazement even in India! Hence, expectedly, for Americans, this was nothing short of a spectacle! While his disciples gave him a warm welcome when he stepped out of the airport, a few natives of the land standing by, ridiculed him for his dressing sense. And, in no time, the number of people ridiculing the saint swelled. Affronted by their behaviour, one of the disciples told Saint Ram, "Ignorant of your accomplishments, these people are mocking you for your sense of dressing. It offends us to watch you being disrespected thus."

On hearing his disciple, saint Ram said, "Perhaps, even saint Ram may not like it, but honestly speaking, I am enjoying this spectacle a lot. Just look at poor saint Ram! He thinks himself to be so wise, but he is not even aware of the kind of attire he should be wearing while travelling to a foreign country!"

Saint Ram's reply astounded his disciples. It was beyond their comprehension who this 'Saint Ram' was and who this 'I' was! A few disciples even wondered, if perhaps, saint Ram had lost his mental equilibrium because of the mockery and affront!

Nevertheless, saint Ram was a pure witness. And a true witness not only enjoys the mess created by others but also the mess created by his own system and even the subsequent confusions that arise. So, just distance yourself a little from your system and see, how a fountain of joy will burst forth, one that will neither abate nor cease ever. For then, you shall be able to witness the foolhardiness indulged in by your own system as well as that of others.

The Great Teaching of a Fakir

The root cause of all your sorrows is desire.
And desire stems from seeking things
in the external world.
In other words, one who is
focussed on his inner self
will never be despondent.

Once upon a time, a stubborn youth wandering in search of knowledge happened to reach a fakir's abode. The first day was spent well, but on the second day when his training began, the fakir gave him just one instruction, "Sit under this tree in solitude and let the thoughts that arise in your mind, flow without interruption. When you get tired of sitting under the tree and wish to stand up, then do so. When you feel hungry, eat and when you feel sleepy, go to sleep; when you feel like taking a walk, go for a walk, and in the interim, if any question comes to your mind, then come to me."

Confounded, the disciple could not understand what to infer from this statement, but as it was his guru's instruction, he began to flow along with his psychological happening. For two days, he was able to follow his guru's instructions. But on the third day, unable to contain his curiosity, he approached the fakir and asked him, "I did as I was told, but for how long should I continue doing so? I have come here to gain knowledge, after all."

The fakir replied, "What you say is indeed right, but this is all I know. Also, I must tell you that there exists no other knowledge apart from learning how to flow with one's psychology. And by the way, did you face any difficulty in the past two days?"

The disciple replied, "Well...No! I didn't!"

The fakir then asked, "Fine, then tell me, did you experience a renewed sense of vigour during these two days?"

Taken aback at the question, the disciple paused for a moment and recalled the past two days. Reviewing his state of being, he realised that in the past two days his energy had indeed grown by leaps and bounds. He immediately fell at the fakir's feet and said, "Truly in the past two days, I faced no problems at all; on the contrary, my energy levels have grown exponentially."

The fakir said, "Then why do you need knowledge in the first place? Tell me, where do you think knowledge is needed in life? The very aim of knowledge is to liberate you of all problems and suffering. And the virtue of knowledge is to equip a human being with renewed vigour. And both these are possible at the same time only by living in accordance with one's psychological happening. Just think, had you not wished to gain knowledge, what all would have happened during the course of these two days? With every wish fulfilled, you would have already become King. Because in the past two days, apart from this one desire for knowledge, everything was happening as per your wish. In other words, had this one desire not been existent, you would have already attained the pinnacle of joy."

A Simple Experiment to Banish Delusion

Ingrain this law in your mind:
the stronger one's 'witness' is,
the faster one's worries and sorrows
shall dissipate.

Let me reiterate, you are the Soul - a pure witness! You are a mere spectator who only watches the play unfold. You are neither a body, nor does any part of the body belong to you. Indeed, it is easy to state this, but how can one believe it? How can this truth be experienced? How can we break the age-old and deep-rooted delusion of identifying oneself with the body? But come what may, this delusion will have to be shattered at any cost because without doing so, one can neither expect one's life to become legendary, nor will one's stress and anxiety dissipate. It is the law that the extent to which one's witness becomes strong, his worries and miseries shall dissipate to that extent. This is because the very root of your problems is your delusion that you are a body, that has a particular name, caste or religion, or one that has his own name, fame and wealth! If this defines your way of existence in the world, then anguish is bound to follow. Because none of these can remain constant; they will always have their ups and downs. And as you consider them your own, you shall inevitably be influenced by every up and down that takes place in them. Moreover, all your learnings are propelling you to strengthen your perception that you are a body. All teachings are inciting you to act on the physical level and in turn propel your body to do one thing or the other. In that case, how can the delusion of considering yourself the body be dispelled? So, if you are wise enough, at least develop the insight to realise and identify the wrong teachings you have trapped yourself in. I have dropped a strong hint here; now, what remains to be seen is, who would be able to free himself of these delusionary teachings and how soon.

Nevertheless, presently, you need to understand that even if you are not able to permanently dwell in the state of being a 'witness', it is alright. But at least try to practise the experiment I am suggesting here to free yourself of this delusion. For, in order to make your life great, you have no option but to weaken this delusion. To be constantly gripped by sorrows, worries and fear can certainly not be called life. Hence, before going to sleep, daily, sit alone with your eyes closed and recall the events that transpired throughout the day. You would realise that you have endured with absolute seriousness all that has happened during the day, considering it to be your own. Subsequently, you have borne the jolts of both pleasure and pain. But no problem! At least free yourself from these upheavals before sleeping. For example, if I have suffered some loss, then I should think that the loss was borne by 'Deep' i.e. as a third person. What do I stand to lose? I am the witness who watched 'Deep' bear the loss and also saw him unnecessarily suffer the resultant pain of that loss. But I am not Deep, so why should 'I' needlessly worry? In case of a quarrel or an insult by someone, I should reflect upon it with a detached approach and think, it was 'Deep' who was insulted, not me! Why should I carry that anger or anguish to sleep? I am not 'Deep', after all! I was just the spectator who watched Deep being unnecessarily insulted and him feeling anguish for no reason. Why should it matter to me—the witness?

With consistent practice, you shall begin to sleep peacefully. And when the sleep is peaceful, you shall wake up to a beautiful dawn. Thereupon, in the same peaceful state of mind, sit in solitude for five minutes again in the morning and repeat the affirmation; the course of action taken by Deep during the day shall be of Deep's. So, let him perform them, and let Deep bear the consequences of those actions as per his state of mind. I shall only watch this show. For, I am just a witness to the show put up by Deep through the day. Just by dedicating these five minutes to yourself, you shall feel light throughout the day. And when you constantly remain peaceful and light, you shall eventually get into this habit. And soon, you shall find yourself closer to the 'witness'. Moreover, the nearer you get to your witness, the more attuned you will be to the secret forces of Nature. This entire process is automatic, which demands no effort from your end. In other words, through this one practice, not only shall your sorrows and worries abate, but you shall also lead a more fruitful life, attaining newer heights. I hope you shall be able to spare at least these fifteen minutes for yourself daily.

Soul
The Laboratory of Truth

If you are repeatedly perturbed
by external circumstances,
know with certainty
that your 'Soul' is still slumbering;
it has not awakened.

The creation of Nature is so designed that a human's Soul is well aware of the entire play of the system. This is the reason, any person, while indulging in a wrongful act, is well aware that the act he is committing is not right! And in fact, this is the one and only barometer for a person to determine whether the act he is indulging in is right or wrong. Soul is the one and only laboratory for judging the truth-untruth of a human being. But still, propelled by selfish interests, a human being very easily disregards his Soul. Why? This is because instead of adhering to right-wrong upheld by his conscience, he accords more importance to his illusory worldly existence. However, one must ingrain it in mind that one who disregards the voice of his conscience will continue to be gripped by sorrows, stress and fear.

It is a common experience that a human, driven by delusion and greed, disregards his Soul. But it becomes worrisome when a human, under the influence of the so-called good-bad, virtue-sin imbibed from the external world, constantly ignores the voice of his Soul. This is even more dangerous! Because, in this situation, he is disregarding his Soul as well as strengthening this false belief on the basis of innumerable lofty arguments from the scriptures and the society. This is the reason why a human being is not able to persecute other humans for the fulfilment of his own selfish interests with the same ease with which he persecutes them in the name of protecting his religion. The same extends to both social beliefs and traditions as well; under the pretext of preserving them, a human persecutes other people with great ease. I hope, with this, you shall comprehend how dangerous are the classifications of virtue-sin and good-bad acquired and adopted from the external world.

Well, presently, let us return to the topic of the supreme power of the Soul. And the essence of all that has been discussed in this context so far is, the Soul, in spite of being a pure witness, has a powerful and clear voice. It is so finely tuned with Nature that when a human indulges in a wrong act, it immediately sends a warning signal and cautions him about his wrongdoing. But, man, consumed by his selfishness, disregards the voice of the Soul and the realisation it aims to bring in its wake. This is the reason I have reiterated umpteen times that a man need not look on the outside to decide the course of his actions—that is, what he should do or not do. His Soul is omniscient and at the time of any wrongdoing, it surely makes him realise his folly. Thus, a man must not disregard the voice of his Soul. This is the one and only barometer to measure any truth; the classification of acts as good-bad, sin-virtue as suggested by external sources is not the correct barometer. On the contrary, misled by such erroneous barometers, a human indulges in wrongdoing with greater ease and a sense of righteousness. Hence, anyone, who trusts the voice of his Soul to weigh right or wrong more than externally gained knowledge, shall easily be able to progress in the right direction. In the process, gradually, his witness shall also awaken, and simultaneously his connect with Nature will also be strengthened.

I shall now explain the same with the reference of the Gita. Arjuna refuses to fight the war. Why? Firstly, because he is gripped by fear, or in other words, he is gripped by his selfish interests; and secondly, he is reeling under the influence of the scriptures which state that kin-killing is a sin. Whereas, Krishna explains to him, "You are not a body, but a Soul. Hence, you must renounce all your selfish interests." Additionally, Krishna also explains to him that the decision of right-wrong stems from the Soul, and not from external knowledge. For, in this spontaneously flowing Nature, new situations are arising every moment. Under the circumstances, only the awakened Soul of a human being is aware of the time, situation and the circumstance behind each event and occurrence, and it is purely on this basis that a decision stems forth from the Soul. "Arjuna, if you, too, wish to arrive at the right decision, then seek refuge in your Soul and the Soul alone. As soon as you seek refuge in it, you will be equipped and prepared to fight the war. Because, your Soul is well aware of the fact that in the present time, situation and circumstance, fighting the war is the best option for you." In essence, Soul is the one and only barometer available to a human being to determine right and wrong. For, only the Soul is aware of what is 'right' and what is 'wrong'; no outer knowledge can be of any help in this. This is the reason why all the external knowledge always proves to be misleading. For, there cannot be any rule of thumb to decide 'what should be done and what should not be done'. What is right at this moment can be wrong in the very next moment.

All in all, you must simply realise that if 'you' do wrong, 'you' shall have to suffer its consequences. And as long as you disregard the Soul, you shall be indulging in wrong acts. And I have already mentioned, a human, under the delusion of considering the system as his own and entangled in the externally acquired classifications of good-bad and virtue-sin disregards his Soul often, for his selfish interests. However, if you wish to become great, then you have no option but to listen to the voice of your Soul; only then shall you stop indulging in wrong acts. And if you wish to listen to the voice of your Soul, then along with your selfishness, you shall also have to get rid of the influences of external knowledge. Now, I have suggested the path; further, it is up to you to both awaken the art of listening to the voice of the Soul as well as to muster the courage to follow that voice and act accordingly to achieve greatness in life.

The Soul is Akin to a Movie Screen

In a movie, what difference does it make whether one plays the role of Rama or Ravana? In a movie, the question is not of playing the role of a protagonist or an antagonist; the question is, how effectively you have played the role ...the same is the case with the 'witness'.

Everyone must have had the experience of going to a cinema hall to watch a film. Some films are made on various social or religious subjects, whereas some are based on violence and negative themes. However, an important fact to note here is, despite the various genres of movies shown on the same screen—be it a religious film or a movie replete with violence and gore—the screen remains unaffected by it. The screen neither becomes sacred when a religious movie is played on it, nor does it become impure if a violent movie is projected on it. Neither is the screen suffused with pride when a religious movie is played on it, nor does it need to be purified with holy water after a violent movie has been projected on it.

Plainly speaking, why should it matter to the screen what sort of a movie is being played on it?! That should be the concern of the movie-maker and the artists involved in the project. When the screen has no role to play in the making or playing of the movie, why should it harbour any feelings of pride or guilt? The only role of a screen is to provide a medium for the movie to play. Even so, the screen is all-important for a movie. For, without a screen, the movie can neither be played nor watched. In other words, despite the screen having no role in the making of the movie and having no part to play in the movie, no movie can be played without the screen.

Now, in view of the above-stated facts, I shall elucidate the Soul using the analogy of a movie screen. The human Soul is akin to a screen on which the life of a human being, made with his own *karma* is played. And mind you, the Soul has no role to play in the making of this movie of human life. Nature—the director of this movie of life—keeps directing it according to the *karmas* of the human being. Then, it does not matter in the least to the Soul, whether this movie is good or bad, resounding with success or overwhelmed by suffering. For the Soul, the brain, ego, mind, body, senses, etc. are just characters in this movie, who, with their mutual co-operation and co-ordination, run this movie continuously. So, let them run it! Let them do what pleases them and let them make any movie to their liking and play it. Let Nature reward them or punish them according to the movie made and played by them; how does it matter to the Soul? It just has to play the role of a screen for the movie to run. And this is all a Soul does! Then in this movie, sometimes, the brain plays the role of a villain and the mind of a hero, while at other times, it is vice versa. Sometimes, the mind and brain behave as lovers, and at other times, there is a bitter face-off between the two akin to that of two people who can't stand each

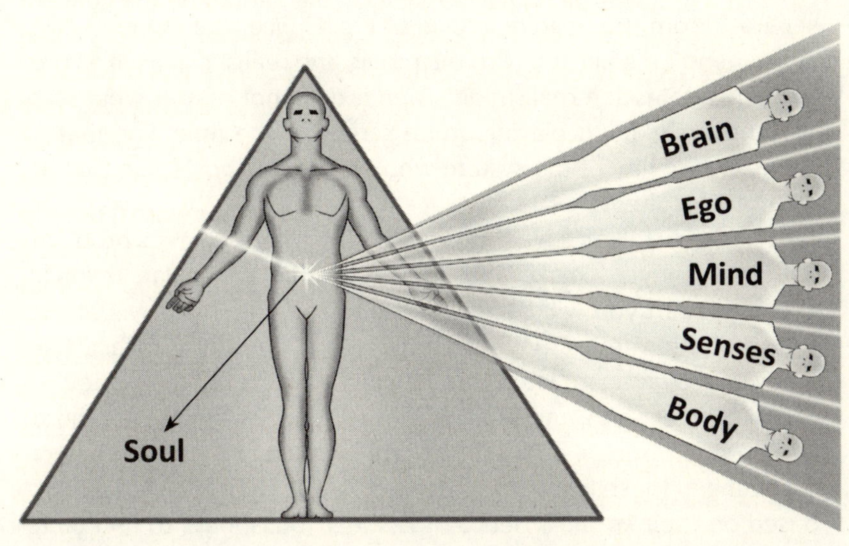

Soul is Like a Movie Screen

For the Soul, the brain, ego, mind, body, senses etc.
are just characters in a movie,
who, with their mutual co-operation
and co-ordination, run this movie continuously.

other. So what? Let each of them do as they please; this is not at all the problem of the Soul. The Soul was, is and will forever remain a screen on which the movie of life is played.

The crux of the matter is, the Soul is different from what life is. Just as the screen is different from the movie, the Soul is separate from the ongoing movie of life. Hence, the moment one stops identifying himself with the movie and realises himself as the Soul, he attains self-realisation. Then it does not matter what sort of a movie i.e. life is playing on his screen at the time. For, that is the responsibility of the system who makes the movie and that of Nature who directs it.

Thus, talks such as 'improve the movie', 'there is a problem with the movie' 'make the movie in this particular manner and only then you will be religious and only then you will attain self-realisation', etc. amount to nothing but ignorance. In fact, this world is a gigantic movie studio in which billions of lifelike-movies are playing at the same time. But in spite of its epic scale, there is only one director of these movies—Nature. All the characters unfolding in these life movies are just playing their individual roles based on their *karmas*. Hence, it is sheer foolishness to find fault in a character who is just playing his part. He would be at fault only if he stopped playing his part and tried to play someone else's part. And unfortunately, this is what everyone is trying to do. In the name of religion and society, these are the teachings imparted to people all over the world. This is the reason why people are at fault for leaving their part and playing someone else's. For this very reason, a human is deprived of wisdom and self-realisation.

Hence, as soon as possible, banish the delusion that you are the movie. It is but ignorance to think there is a problem in your life-movie or that there is a need to improve it. The truth is, you are not the movie. And if you are not the movie, how does it matter to you what sort of a movie it is? The moment you firmly comprehend this, that very moment your life-movie shall become Nature's movie. That's about it! Then in the blink of an eye, Nature shall make this movie so marvellous that not just you, but the entire world shall look on in awe.

Well, there is yet another point to grasp here, that if the Soul is different from the movie, there is no denying that it is different! If the Soul is not the movie, then it certainly is not. Hence, irrespective of the kind of movie being played, the sanctity and purity of the Soul remains intact. Under all circumstances, its innocence remains unsullied. This is the reason when even the vilest person comes closer to the witness, his pure innocence comes to the fore instantly, even if it is for just a split second. And this is also the reason, for a wise being, there is no difference between a sinner and a virtuous person. For, the actual form of both is the 'Soul'. No matter what one does, deep inside, he is pure and innocent. The poor being is only playing his role. In view of this, when Arjuna speaks of sin-virtue, Krishna propounds that for a wise person, there is actually no difference between a dog, an elephant, an outcast (pariah), or a humble Brahmin (priest). For him, all are one because in the end, all of them are but playing their own roles. Hence, do not indulge in ignorant talks of labelling one as 'virtuous' or 'sinful'. Understand my clear definition of a sinner; the one who refuses to play his role in life-movie is a sinner, and if you too, resort to lofty, useless arguments and refrain from playing your role, then you too, shall become a sinner.

In short, I have stated the truth as clearly as possible. Only the ignorant speak of sin-virtue and good-bad. Egoistic people impart teachings about 'what to do' and 'what not to do'. The wise say only one thing – Wake up...! Awaken...! You are not the movie; you are the screen! That is the end of story!

Soul is *Praann* (life-energy)

The screen is merely the medium
for the movie to play;
the same is the role of your 'witness'
in your life.

Now answer my question – When can a movie play and for how long? As long as there exists a screen! Right?! Without a screen, no movie in this world can be played even for a moment. Likewise, the 'Soul' too is a screen for the movie of life to play on. The movie of life shall continue to play only till the Soul dwells in the body. No sooner does the Soul leave the body, than the movie stops playing. In other words, this Soul is the *Praann* or life-energy of the human being.

But as the Soul is beyond the realm of Time and Space, it is beyond the reach of science. Scientific consciousness is not evolved enough, nor has it made enough progress to be able to fathom the world that exists beyond the realm of Time and Space. In fact, science is in a state of ignorance, even with reference to the source

The Soul is *Praann* (life-energy)

The movie of life shall continue to play
only till the Soul dwells in the body.
No sooner does the Soul leave the body,
than the movie stops playing.
In other words, this Soul is the *Praann*
or life-energy of the human being.

of happiness or the root cause of sorrow. Such being the case, the Soul is far beyond the reach of science. Science holds a limited understanding with reference to life that if the heart has stopped beating, and the brain is dead, then the person is pronounced dead.

However, since I am explaining various concepts in scientific parlance taking science as my base, science too shall have to work in tandem with spiritual science sooner or later. And the day when these two become a cohesive whole, the world shall have answers to all questions. Honestly speaking, my very aim behind these efforts is to unite these two and I sincerely hope that my effort shall bear fruit soon. Nevertheless, for now, you must etch it in your mind that in spite of being nothing or doing nothing, the Soul is the be-all and end-all for you. It is your very *Praann*, your life-energy. It is because of its presence that your life-movie is still playing. No sooner it leaves the body, than the game shall be over. But surprisingly, even then, you do not accord it due importance. Isn't that amazing?! Nevertheless, it's high time you stop performing such wonders!

Witness – "The System is not My Concern!"

You are just a pure 'witness'.
The realisation that the body, mind or senses do not belong to you, is wisdom.
And that is why, the wise never interfere with any of them. The entire ruckus about suppressing the body, mind and senses has been created by ignoramuses.

I am sure, you must have grasped it well by now that the witness and the system are two separate entities. The 'system' implies the sum total of your mind, brain, ego, body and senses, and you are not the 'system'. In any case, you were, you are and you shall always remain a pure witness. But unfortunately, here, a majority of people have believed themselves to be the system. However, this is nothing but ignorance, a 'Maya' or delusion, and this is the reason everyone's life is entangled in problems. One who wants to save himself from problems shall surely have to get closer to his 'witness' i.e. his Soul. There is no other remedy to eliminate the problems of life. You may try several other formulas, but your sorrows and pain shall not abate. Know this as a law that the closer one gets to his witness, the newer heights one's life shall begin to scale. However, getting closer to the witness is not as easy as it sounds. This is because 'old habits die hard' and the habit of identifying oneself with the system is age-old.

This, in turn, gives rise to the question – Why is a human being so deluded about himself? There is only one reason for this—in the history of mankind, the ratio of the ignoramuses far surpasses the wise ones. Hence, if there have been fifty wise people, then the ignorant ones have run into millions. And these ignorant people have had no idea about the Soul; they themselves have been ensnared in the delusion of the system and even then, they keep harping on their knowledge. Now, the one for whom knowledge stems from the 'system', who imparts knowledge as a 'system', would obviously provide knowledge to the 'system'. And, pray what knowledge can be imparted to the system, except for, giving instructions on which act to indulge in and which to abstain from! Now, the ignorant people do not understand, that in an attempt to indulge in an act or refrain from indulging in an act, the witness is dying a slow death. Here, I have stated the most profound truth pertaining to human life. So now, it's your turn to kindle your intelligence and immediately break free from all delusory knowledge, beginning today, now and here itself!

Nevertheless, presently, let us continue our discussion on the digression of humans and the teachings of the ignorant. Unfortunately, a human being is more attracted to nonsensical knowledge provided to the system and by the 'system'. And then on the basis of this knowledge, he makes extensive use of his system. And the more one makes use of the system, the more one gets trapped. This is because the more a person uses the system, the more he continues to be distanced from his Soul. And the extent to which one is distanced from one's Soul, is the extent to which he is perturbed. This is an immutable law! How much more explicit can I be? However, at present, simply understand that it is the knowledge of whether to indulge in an act or not that is wreaking havoc in human life. This is because as soon as a human indulges in an act or refrains from indulging in an act, his 'witness' becomes weak. Unfortunately, the ignorance among people at large is so overbearing that now, the fact that everything can be accomplished by mere 'witnessing' is beyond their comprehension.

Yet another significant fact for people to comprehend is, oftentimes, a human being, functioning under this delusion, either does a lot or restrains himself from doing a lot that he can do. As it is generally believed that an individual who has reached close to the Soul is as perfect as one can be as per religious and social standards. Now, billions of humans are living in adherence to parameters of society and religion, so have they all reached closer to their Souls?! Not at all! Please check, perhaps a handful of them might be closer to the Soul, but in general, none of them have anything to do with the Soul. The omniscient Soul is so potent and powerful that you cannot even imagine.

However, presently, you must understand that an individual, who has come close to the Soul, shall never abide by conventional beliefs and teachings. Why would the Soul give importance to religions and societies that are just two to five thousand years old, whereas the Soul is the force through which this entire universe has come into existence? And since we are on the subject of the Soul, I shall only ask you to stop measuring humans who are living close to their Souls, on the scales of your baseless limiting beliefs such as 'a human living close to his Soul wanders in the forest, practises penance and is a staunch believer or renounces wealth and splendour'. These beliefs have been thrust upon you by so-called religions and societies who are blinded by ignorance. I have nothing to do with them. It is their choice to continue propagating the beliefs they want to spread, and live by the beliefs they like. When a human being is free from Nature's side to either salvage or degrade himself, then why should I engage myself in reasoning with those who are hell-bent on destroying themselves?! I am only worried about the bright, talented humans who still have the potential and possibility in them to get close to the Soul and lay the foundation for a wonderful life. Moreover, I am not someone who beats around the bush. And why should I? I neither wish to amass wealth, nor do I wish to open a hermitage, nor do I wish to earn fame and honour. I have nothing to do with all these illusory achievements. With Nature's grace, I have so much work to do in the form of writing and speaking that I have no spare time for anything else. Whether good or bad, I am satisfied with however Nature has made me. This is indeed a matter of great contentment for me that I am diligently able to perform the task assigned to me by Nature, and along with it, I am also able to indulge in my hobbies and passions. And I wish to spread this very contentment around. I am cognisant of the truth that there is no God other than the beating heart of a human being. My incessant efforts, therefore, are dedicated towards making every heart beat with joy. As I am content with how Nature has made me, I am bound by none but Nature. And when I am not bound by anything, why should I beat around the bush? I shall speak and do only that which is conveyed and commanded to me by Nature. I shall continue with my efforts to dispel the ignorance that prevails among humans in every possible manner. I shall continue explaining the truths that are requisites in building a great life. As a matter of fact, my views are more relevant and useful for those few million humans whose Souls are awakened at least to some extent.

Hence, you must grasp well what I am now about to explain. Never look for the seeker of the Soul in the confined parameters of so-called religions and societies, and also do not make the mistake of construing yourself spiritually enlightened on that premise. The human system, however it is, has been received by a man according to his *karmas* spanning several past births. And the sole authority over this system lies with Nature alone. Believing the system to be one's own and subsequently experimenting with it in various ways shall only lead one astray, especially, considering the fact that this is not what a witness will ever do. A witness is well aware that when the system does not belong to him, then why should he ask it to act in a certain way, do a certain thing, or even refrain from doing anything. For, he thinks it is the matter concerning the system and He who runs it; not me for sure. I shall just watch their internal games. If the system has some faults, then let the one who has built the system, rectify it. How does it matter to me? I am certainly not endowed with powers that enable me to rectify the system. Alas! What is my standing in this large colossal play of Nature that I can effectuate something positive? This is the knowledge and state of mind of the seeker. And only a person living with such clarity in mind is able to realise and experience the witness to some extent. Such a person has faith in both the Almighty, and the system the Almighty has designed for him. Besides, he lives in acceptance of the positives and negatives of his system that has been built on the basis of his past *karmas*; and only he is a truly religious person. Indeed, how can a person consider himself a believer—having faith in God—if he is unable to entrust his system to God, and instead desires to decide for himself what his system should be like. Such a person has, in fact, become an egoist. His expression is explicitly that of challenging God and stating that the system built by Him is faulty.

Unfortunately, the world is mired with such egoists who keep tampering with their systems and simultaneously talk of having faith in God. Needless to say, all such people, without exception, are distressed in life. And behind this lie many secret forces of Nature; once you fathom all the secret forces of Nature one by one, gradually you shall begin to grasp this science in its totality. To reiterate, understand once again that when the system does not belong to me; when it has been given to me by Nature, then who am I to term it good or bad? Who am I to improve it or corrupt it? If you comprehend this, then your life shall take a quantum leap right here, right now. But I know the helplessness of a human and can well understand his predicament too. Humans are so bogged down by wrong teachings and beliefs that although this appears very easy when read or heard, actually, it is very difficult to implement. But once you begin to grasp it, everything shall fall in place and soon, Nature shall take you in its fold.

However, for now, let us again return to the point that I wish to elucidate, that a human living in close proximity to the Soul is always unpredictable; he can do anything, everything or nothing. But he will certainly not fit within the parameters of conventional beliefs, no matter what. Having said that, although the world shall weigh you on the scales of its beliefs and also label you as good or bad on that premise, do not pay heed to them and get caught in the trap. You must understand that you are answerable to your Soul alone, not to the world. You are answerable only to the Supreme Soul of this universe. So, do not worry if the world labels you as bad. Just save yourself from falling in the eyes of God. For, that is the only way you shall be saved. The world has not just abused the spiritually enlightened ones, but has also harassed and cruelly persecuted them. Nobody has been an exception to this, right from Buddha and Krishna to Kabir and Meera. The same so-called religions and societies have crucified Jesus and poisoned Socrates. So, do not pay heed to this insane world, rather just focus on moving closer to your Soul.

The one who is a witness of himself can do anything. He is not a slave to anything.

I am stating all this because many of those termed bad or vile by the world are actually living their life in close proximity to the Soul. On the other hand, the Souls of many, honoured and respected by the same world, are lying dormant, as the world is not aware of any secret, either of the Soul or that of Nature. And when the people close to the Soul make progress, lead a content life and become great and famous, the same world pronounces that such people have achieved progress through wicked means. In other words, they begin to think that progress has no connection with goodness. They do not understand that in the eyes of the secret forces of Nature, the one who is close to the Soul, who interferes the least with his system, and who just flows along with whatever is stemming forth from the system is actually good. And it is only such people who progress in life on a daily basis. It is only their peace of mind and happiness that continues to grow manifold by the day. And as the world is not able to digest this, it just keeps venting out its frustration by talking ill about such people who are living in sheer bliss. And I am stating all this just to encourage these very people. So, out of kindness to themselves, such people living in peace and bliss must not fall prey to this delusion prevalent in the world. In fact, I shall provide a few tests for such people so that they can check themselves on the parameters of these tests, rather than following the deluded worldly barometers. Once you do so, you will instantly realise where you stand at the level of Soul.

Moving further, you need to comprehend that the so-called religions, societies and worlds that you speak of, can never accept any act or action of Krishna, the man who married eight times, who loved multiple women, who indulged in *raasa* (dancing with abandon) with the *gopis*, who deceived and cheated, who lied blatantly, who slayed people and fought wars. But what can such poor people do? In the Gita, Krishna has declared himself as the God of all Gods with such magnificence that these hapless beings cannot even rebut Krishna. Thus, they feel compelled to worship Him. Funnily enough, if a person appears to be indulging in acts similar to those of Krishna's, then these very people do not hesitate even for a second before pronouncing him a sinner. Now what can those having such ignorance and double standards be expected to know about the Soul and the secret forces of Nature? If you are wise, then you should at least be able to grasp this bit. You must also clearly understand that in his entire life, Krishna never indulged in any wrong deed even for a moment. Whatever he did, and whenever he did, it was just perfect. That is why, I have penned the entire life journey of Krishna in *'I am Krishna'*. In this book, I have attached far more importance to the purpose behind Krishna's actions rather than just providing an account of his acts and actions. This is because, in my view, Krishna is the only personality, by understanding whom, all confusions regarding 'what one must do' and 'what one must not do' can come to an end.

In a nutshell, I am explaining all this because I am more concerned for those who have saved themselves from the prevalent ignorance and have reached closer to their Souls. I don't want them to be perturbed by the false certificates issued upon them by the deluded world and digress from their path. I also wish to help those who still have the possibility of moving closer to their Souls. Otherwise, I always bow to those with folded hands who are stubborn, egoistic and enslaved by their wrong beliefs. And, this bowing simply denotes that now, there is no possibility that any knowledge or God can help them. Let them be content in harassing the likes of Buddha, Kabir, Christ and Meera, and worship them when they bid adieu to this world; as far as we are concerned, we neither have to honour nor dishonour them. We just have to learn from the lives of these great Souls and their teachings, imbibe them into our lives and lead our lives on the path to achieve greatness.

I shall now provide some scientific tests to assess how close or far one is from his Soul. First, comprehend these parameters and then assess yourself on the suggested parameters. Thereupon, focus on aligning yourself with these parameters as much as possible. And from now onwards, begin to assess others purely on the basis of these tests. Get close to the one who appears to pass the test and distance yourself from the one failing the test. This is because life is meant to be lived, and it is better to live one's life in the company of true seekers. If you are in the company of wrong people, you shall have to suffer a lot on their account, too. And, I have seen a majority of people being doubly punished thus.

They certainly suffer on their own account, but more importantly, they gravely suffer because of the pain emanating from wrong relationships too.

Hence, you must carefully comprehend each test in depth; consider this to be the most important test of your life. And, if you find yourself perfectly in sync with the parameters mentioned below, then proceed without any hesitation or worry. You can rest assured, for, Nature is holding your hand and guiding you forward. And as they say in India, *Jaako Raakhe Saaiyaan Maar Sake Na Koi*, i.e. nobody can harm the one who is protected by God. So, be close to God and not the world. Nonetheless, in the end, I would also request you to never try to balance the two. God and society–both can never be balanced at a time.

Tests to Measure Your Proximity to the Soul

'The more stable and steadfast we are,
the closer we are to the Soul.
It is our fretting over the good and the bad
which has kept us at a distance from our Soul.'
For the sensible ones,
the 'difference between knowledge and ignorance'
comes clear with this single aphorism.

I shall now reveal the tests that can help one understand how close or far one is from the Soul, that is to say, at what level one is living with regards to the Soul. As far as human beings are concerned, this knowledge is extremely significant, as the closer a person is to his Soul, the faster he would progress on the path of his destiny. And only those who are traversing the path of destiny can be termed fortunate. On the other hand, the more distant one is from the Soul, the more one would be treading in the direction opposite to his destiny; and these people are called the 'unfortunate' ones. Let me clarify that this is the one and only definition of being 'fortunate' and 'unfortunate'. As for the rest, Nature has nothing to do with your superficial, irrelevant and baseless definitions. If you wish to comprehend the secrets of destiny in entirety, then read the book on Destiny penned by me. However, presently, you must understand that your life shall become beautiful if you pass this test. Also remember, that in order to become great, it is important to be in the company of those who are fortunate. Only you being fortunate is not going to serve the purpose. In order to make your life worthwhile, it is important to be surrounded by fortunate people. If you are living with unfortunate people or those with dormant Souls, then their misfortune shall leave a stench on you as well.

Hence, repeatedly read the criteria that I am providing here, in order to know how close or far you are from the Soul. Weigh yourself accurately on this scale. Endeavour to move closer to these criteria and try to be in sync with them as much as possible. Also, weigh others around you on this scale. And as soon as possible, form a group of people who fit into these criteria. Bear in mind that the closer a person is to his Soul, the more support he will receive from the secret forces of Nature. Remember, these are all immutable laws. Hence, take them seriously and try to abide by them as much as possible.

A) Negativity should not last long

Negativity does not last long in people who are close to their Souls. However, I do not intend to state that they are never gripped by anger, worry or sorrow. They do get gripped by these emotions, but such emotions do not linger for long. For example, you are angry at someone or feel displeased with someone for a certain reason. Now, these are natural reactions so it is fine! But here, you must understand that the closer a person is to his Soul, the faster his anger and displeasure shall dissipate. On the other hand, you

Negativity is Proof of Distance from The Soul

Positivity is the proof of living close to the Soul
and negativity is proof of being distant from the Soul.
Although a person living close to the Soul
gets gripped by emotions like anger, worry and sorrow,
these emotions do not last for long.

must be aware that in some people anger and displeasure could last for months, while there are some amazing specimens in whom anger and displeasure lasts for years; such people have nothing do with the Soul. One, who is close to the Soul, shall become normal in an hour or two. And when I say normal, mind you, absolutely normal! For, there are many who temporarily behave normal owing to circumstances, but later continue venting out their anger and displeasure in fits and starts over the years. In other words, in spite of sporting a normal and calm demeanour on the outside, they are fuming from within. These are all signs of their Souls being dormant and such people can neither be helped nor can they accomplish anything worthwhile in life.

The same applies to the situations of worry and fear in a person. In this case, too, I would not state that those close to the Soul are never gripped by worry and fear. Here, too, the question is, for how long do such emotions last? Rather, an additional question arises in this case—Do the worries pertain to the present or the future? And if these worries and fears pertain to the future, then how far into the future? If one is worried about what would happen a year or two ahead in the future, then it is not a sign of an awakened Soul. And if the time span of worry extends to 10-20 years, then it is even worse. And if you are worrying about reaching heaven and hell, then you might as well consider your Soul dead! When Arjuna speaks of heaven and hell, Krishna says, "Only the ignorant worry about such issues! O Arjuna, in truth, gripped by fear and worry, the suffering you are enduring at present is nothing but hell. In other words, heaven and hell are the present mental state of a human being. If the mind is gripped by negative thoughts and emotions, then it is an instant experience of hell. If the mind is in the fold of positive thoughts and emotions, it is an instant experience of heaven; no other heaven or hell exists." But Arjuna was greatly influenced by the scriptures, whereas Krishna was only concerned about convincing Arjuna to fight the war. Thus, when Arjuna was not able to comprehend Krishna's statements with regards to the mental state of heaven and hell, Krishna instantly changed his stance and said, "Irrespective of what you have grasped so far, know it with certainty that your present thinking is not going to lead you to heaven. For, without changing your current thinking, you shall not be at peace with yourself."

Even so, presently, let us put the Bhagavad Gita aside and return to the current topic, as the discourse in the Gita spanned eighteen chapters. Therefore, with regards to the Soul, one must understand that the farther one's worries and fear extend into the future, the greater is one's distance from the Soul. And those who are in the grip of worry and fear only with reference to the present problems can consider themselves to be aware to a large extent. In other words, worrying about a long time into the future is the sign of a dormant Soul. And you shall surely have to comprehend the complete science behind this aspect of Soul. As stated earlier, I speak only in scientific terms, thus, I believe in proving every point rather than indulging in empty talk.

Therefore, understand what exactly the Soul is; it is just a 'witness'. And as a witness, it is just a spectator to the play of life. For a witness, neither does the body belong to him nor does the lifespan of the body. The one dwelling in the Soul surely knows that he was, he is and he shall always prevail. Hence, he doesn't stand to gain anything or lose anything. He knows that any gain or loss ensued, would be of the body and its life, which he is not concerned with at all! Here, you must understand that why would such a person be gripped by any worry or fear irrespective of what happens to the body or his life? Needless to say, the closer one is to the Supreme Soul, the lesser he shall be gripped by worries and fear. And if at all some worries grapple him, those will be of the present or at the most, of one or two days into the future. He shall never be gripped by worries or fears of the distant future. And he shall certainly not be gripped by worries or fears of next birth or heaven-hell ever. A 'dormant Soul' simply implies that such a person firmly believes his system and his life to be his own. And this is the reason why he gets so deeply affected by every high and low in life.

Here, I have given a scientific test for determining one's closeness or distance from the Soul. To become serious in every matter is a proof that one is leading life considering the system to be one's own. At the same time, not to be highly concerned, irrespective of what happens, is a proof of being close to the witness. Hence, check yourself on the basis of this criterion. If you are gripped by deep fears and worries regarding your family or your future, then know yourself to be distanced from the Soul. If you feel deeply angered when you are insulted, or when you hear others talking ill about your God or religion, then it implies that your Soul is still in a deep slumber. The proof of this is, it is such people who have killed Christ, Socrates and Mansoor; and it is such people who have persecuted Buddha, Kabir and Meera. And these are the people who have proclaimed themselves to be caretakers of religions and sects. Even by mistake do not construe them as religious.

However, you should forget about them and focus on yourself! Check how much you are gripped by fear and worry. How long do they linger? And if you are gripped by fear and worry of the distant future, then be cautious. Limit your fear and worry to today or tomorrow. By doing so, life-sapping illusions such as worry and fear will be weakened. Have faith that the one who has brought you into existence shall also nurture you with full responsibility. At this point, bear this law in mind, that as soon as you shed your worries, from that very moment, the Almighty takes charge and begins to worry about you. And when the Almighty worries about a person, why should the person have to endure even an iota of negativity within?

Hence, if you are worried about the future of your children, then too, take it as a sign that you are still at a distance from your Soul. The seeker knows that every child is the child of God. And when he does not even have to worry about his own body and life, then why would he worry about his children? He knows that if he worries about his children, then God will be left with nothing to do! What would happen of God's system of justice that functions on automation mode?

Well, I have explained what must be explained. Now, the ball is in your court to grasp and move closer to your Soul. Hopefully, you must have grasped that without inching closer to the Soul, nothing worthwhile shall happen in life. Hence, stop squandering your time and energy in innumerable other avenues as you normally do. Instead, use your time and energy to bridge the gap between yourself and your Soul. The rest will be taken care of by the Almighty, so leave it to him!

B) Anger should be just a pretence

One of the biggest misconceptions that prevails is, the seeker does not get angry. Well, they too, according to the time, circumstance and behaviour of other humans, have to resort to anger. For example, Krishna's life was so complicated that on various instances, he had to demonstrate his furious form before others. In fact, he had demonstrated his furious form even in the Gita. But each time, his anger was exhibited only when it was the need of the hour; in other words, it was a mere act. As soon as the desired outcome was achieved, the anger would dissipate and the very next moment he would be absolutely normal. For, such anger was enacted only to either convey his point to others or to manoeuvre them in the right direction. In other words, the anger, too, in the end, was meant for the benefit of others. And in case of the seeker, this is verily the only form of anger.

On the other hand, any form of anger expressed by an ordinary human being is the reflection of his selfishness and ego. He gets angry when his selfish interests are threatened or when something is said or done against his desire or belief. Why is this so? This is because instead of his Soul, he considers his body, life and beliefs as his own. He is not aware enough to understand that whether it is his body or life, none of them belong to him; they are but instruments of Nature, which Nature uses as a medium to carry out its task. He is ignorant of the fact that he is just a witness in the ongoing play between Nature and his body. Hence, whenever his selfish interest or ego is attacked, he is enraged. Then, from time to time, he vents his anger on the person who he feels, has attacked him.

In essence, you need to understand that the question is not about becoming or not becoming angry. The question is, is one displaying anger out of selfishness or for the good of others? Also, after the display of anger, how soon does one return to his normal self? So, only he should consider himself close to the Soul, who, after becoming angry, returns to his normal self in no time. On the other hand, the longer one's anger lasts, the more distanced he must consider himself from the Soul. And those whose anger lasts for many months and years should clearly understand that their Soul is dormant. They are absolutely clueless about their form as a witness. Their system means everything to them. Such being the case, they have no option but to endure the pain of every blow, for a very long time. And I have to state with great pain that for people with such a mental state, life is akin to death!

Anger is not your problem. Your problem is that anger lingers in you even after it is vented out.

Imagine the level of anger existent in those who have pronounced various cruel punishments in hell for human beings! Look at the quantum of their anger and its span! Well, I would leave them to their own devices. But you should at least feel blessed that you have not distanced yourself from the Soul as much as these people. Then why do you take futile anger and displeasure so seriously and make your present life 'hell'? When the system belongs to Nature, why do you not entrust it to Nature and just enjoy the show?

C) No pride – No shame

Measuring one's sense of pride and shame is the most infallible test to measure one's distance from the Soul. If pride or repentance ensues as a fallout of your action, then know it with certainty that you have not yet become a pure witness. Your Soul has not yet manifested itself in totality. As a matter of fact, the complete manifestation of the Soul is a tall order! Hence, it is okay to be proud about something or to repent an action once in a while. If this occurs just a few times in a year, then you can certainly consider yourself close to the Soul; provided such pride and repentance does not last for long! But, if the pride or repentance lasts for days on end or months, then you must realise that you are still distant from your Soul. And if pride and shame follow after every other instance, then you must know with certainty that at present, you are in a state of deep slumber and your Soul is absolutely dormant. Under the circumstances, there is no difference between you and those pundits, maulvis and priests who indulge in self-aggrandisement by organising huge processions extolling their achievements. Why should one be consumed with so much pride, and for what reason? In order to stroke their ego, they need huge resplendent thrones just for parroting a few lines! Krishna and Buddha worked for the well-being of entire humanity and yet they were never gripped by pride! Even after lighting up the entire world with his invention of the bulb, Edison never puffed with pride! For that matter, did you ever see Bill Gates or Ratan Tata exhibiting any pride?

On the other hand, look at ordinary people! They swell with pride on just buying a new car! And in religious matters, don't even ask! If by chance, they happen to visit a temple, mosque or church, their sense of pride assumes epic proportions. And all these are but signs of being distanced from one's Soul. All pride is but a proof of your unawareness and ignorance. Take for instance the case of the legendary singer, Mohammad Rafi—a voice like his rarely manifests, perhaps once in thousands of years, and yet, how humble he was! Even when someone praised him, he would say, "I have no contribution in this, for, it is all by the grace of Allah! If God so wished, he would have thus graced someone else and that person would have become Rafi!" What Mohammad Rafi said is the truth of the seeker! Those who dwell close to the Soul know that everything great in existence manifests by the grace of Nature. They know, they are mere witnesses to this grace of Nature. They know deep in their hearts that they are just being instrumental in Nature's scheme of things and are thus mere mediums for whatever is happening through them. And know this for certain that only the one, who is close to his Soul, can have such a profound realisation. Being close to the Soul simply implies that I have shed the delusion and stopped considering my system, my body and my life as my own. I have surrendered all of them to Nature. Now, let Nature decide what it wants to accomplish through the system; why should I bother? I will just watch the ongoing play between Nature and this system. And for such a spectator, there is no reason to feel either proud or ashamed irrespective of what the system does. Such pride and shame are harboured by those whose awareness is not yet kindled. Like Arjuna, they too take pride in virtuous acts and fear in the face of sin. Panic they will, for, they have assumed the existence of the system as their own. But as for you, please be kind to yourself and gradually stop considering the system as your own. Surrender the system to Nature and become its instrument. Then you shall feel neither pride nor shame. Imbibe the idea well that what actions one indulges in and what one refrains from, has no relation whatsoever to one's closeness with the Soul. Proximity or distance from the Soul is determined by whether or not one gets gripped by pride or shame after indulging in an action. This is a science and I hope you must have grasped it well. This science is straight and simple—feelings of pride or shame are proof that you are the 'doer' of your actions. On the other hand, absence of pride and shame is proof that the realisation is still alive in you that you are just the medium through which existence is getting everything done; in other words, everything you are doing is at the behest of existence.

If you have still not grasped this, I shall again attempt to explain with the help of an example from Krishna's life. For, as long as you relate the indulgence or non-indulgence of an action with religiousness, you shall continue to deviate from the path of spiritual enlightenment. Do you know what Krishna did after enunciating the greatest scripture of human history—the Bhagavad Gita? He became a part of the epic devastating war of Mahabharata! And what did he do in that war? He lied, he deceived and he breached a promise. Not just this, he even compelled Yudhishthira, who had taken a vow to always speak the truth, to utter a lie. So, did he repent later for having done so? Did he think even once – 'What all have I done after enunciating such an eternal Truth (The Bhagavad Gita)?' 'No'...an emphatic 'No'! That is why, I am asking you to stop indulging in such antics. Comprehend the profundity of these truths and the secret forces of Nature. Do not get mired in the classification of 'good deeds' and 'bad deeds', 'right' and 'wrong'. Free yourselves of these foolish traps laid by the so-called organised religions and society. Let the divine play of Nature decide as to what should be done and what should not be done. Do not engage yourself in the analysis of the righteousness of an action; whether it is good or bad, sin or virtue. Moreover, who are you to analyse the great divine play of Nature anyway?

And, if nothing else, at least begin to comprehend the Bhagavad Gita a bit, which is the greatest scripture to have ever been enunciated. Unfortunately, people have drawn such baseless interpretations of this epic scripture, that they are not even worthy of mention. Even the Gita has been reduced to the role of an adornment or a product used for attracting customers by those who run the business of religion. When, in fact, the Bhagavad Gita is a scripture meant to shut down such shops. It is a flowing stream of truth and a river brimming with pristine knowledge. The Bhagavad Gita brings a man closer to his Soul. It kindles the latent powers of human mind and makes a human being psychologically powerful. Such being the case, how can this great scripture ever be used to run the business of religion?

Well, let the people with dormant Souls draw their own interpretations. The pertinent point for you to grasp here is, primarily, what is the main question posed by Arjuna in the Gita? The question is – What is better, to wage a war or not? Should I fight the war or not? And what is Krishna's reply? Krishna states, "O Arjuna, if you fight and win the war, you shall be gripped with pride. And one day, this pride shall kill you. If you fight and lose the war, then you shall die of sorrow. At the same time, if you run from the battlefield, you shall die of shame. In other words, whatever you do, your defeat is certain, in all three outcomes. Hence, your very question of whether you should fight the war or not is, by itself, wrong. For, if you fight, you may die and even if you flee from the battlefield, you shall still face death eventually. Therefore, if you wish to save yourself, you have only one option—become a witness to the war like me. Along with the body, surrender your fighting skills also to the existence. He shall navigate your system and make you do what has to be done through you. Then, why should you be bothered even if he gets thousands killed through you? Or even if he destroys the entire world using you as the medium of destruction. Believe me, even then you shall not incur an iota of sin! Simply have faith in the truth I have revealed here that a witness can never become a sinner."

In essence, you need to understand that the entire play of life depends on the fact that to what extent you consider the system as your own and to what extent you consider it that of the Almighty. If you consider it to be that of the Almighty, then whatever the system does, you need not repent or swell with pride. You tend to be gripped by all these feelings only when you consider the system to be your own. And the more one has identified himself with the system, the more he would feel proud and ashamed on a daily basis. No matter what, such people shall always remain in pain and suffer from within. And in my view, to experience such painful, agonising emotions and to live a life fraught with pain and sorrows is the greatest sin a human is committing against his own self.

D) Firmness in actions is important

In the Gita, Krishna says, "O Arjuna, Soul is the force that provides absolute firmness to your actions. In other words, all actions of the seeker are performed with absolute firmness. Firmness here implies lack of doubts; no confusion whatsoever while performing an action. Moreover, one must understand that the more one is confused, the more one is distanced from the Soul. For, Nature is an infinite play, seamlessly flowing without a pause for even a moment. And where there is no pause, how can there be confusion? Have you ever seen the sun in a state of confusion? Just imagine what would happen if the earth were to stop rotating for a moment in a state of confusion! Humans would become extinct in no time!"

Therefore, Krishna is saying, "Arjuna, a seeker does not have even an iota of confusion about anything. Your extremely confused state is a proof that in the present moment, you have moved far away from your Soul. But trust me, the Supreme Soul is very well a part of each action performed with absolute firmness. Since you are concerned only about the battle of Mahabharata, let me tell you; even if you are the worst of sinners, but are absolutely firm (in your actions), you shall be construed as *dharmatma* - a saint. This is because firmness and confusion are the only parameters to be weighed on the scales of the Supreme Soul. Arjuna, you must know that absolute firmness in actions is possible only in the case of a person flowing along with Nature. A digressed person will do everything half-heartedly. Such a person can never be fully absorbed in his actions. He shall always be worried about the results."

In the same vein, Krishna further says, "O Arjuna, you must also understand, that all these confusions are arising from duality in the human mind. As long as a human continues to weigh actions

Perform Your Action Without Worrying about its Result

Maintain firmness in each action. Eventually, there comes a day when that firmness is manoeuvred in the right direction by Nature. The very meaning of firmness is absence of worry about the result. If you worry about the result, then you will never be able to complete any task with due firmness and concentration.

on the dual scales of sin-virtue, good-bad, gain-loss, yours-mine, one's own-others, he will remain confused about every action. For, until then, he shall continue making decisions on the basis of these dualities. And as long as he continues to make decisions himself, he will continue to firmly consider the system as his own. Contrary to this, why would the seeker, who is not considering the system as his own, be caught in the dualities of sin-virtue, good-bad or gain-loss etc. and become confused about indulging or not indulging in an action? He continues to perform all actions that ought to be performed through him with firmness, without worrying about sin-virtue or gain-loss. It is a law that the less confusion one has, the closer he would be to the Soul, because lesser confusion implies greater firmness in his action. On the other hand, dormant is the Soul of the one who is confused about everything."

The one who lacks fortitude can never achieve anything in life.

In a nutshell, you need to grasp that firmness is a miraculous virtue. It straightaway takes the human closer to his Soul. Hence, when actions are performed with firmness, without worrying about the result, the nature of the action or the action per se does not matter at all. And this is a profound science. I shall elucidate the same with the example of sage Valmiki, a popular character from the epic Ramayana. Before attaining sainthood, he would openly loot people with absolute firmness and never had an iota of confusion regarding the nature of his actions, whether they were right or wrong. Even though the act was of looting, his contentment was paramount. The scientific aspect of this act which needs to be grasped is, such firmness just needs to be manoeuvred in the right direction. And see for yourself, as soon as he found the right direction, he became the great sage Valmiki.

Well, this is a very ancient tale of Indian mythology, hence, I shall now endeavour to explain this with the help of a contemporary example. Everyone is well aware of how mischievous the world-renowned founder of Apple, Steve Jobs was as a child. However, for him, his actions or pranks were by no means wrong. In other words, he was firm in his actions. One day, his school teacher, Hill, gave his firmness the right direction. Can you imagine what happened next? As soon as his firmness found the right direction, he became the world renowned, Steve Jobs. This is exactly what Krishna explains to Arjuna – "Time and again, you are asking me about the virtues of a *Dharmatma* – a *saint*! So, listen! Like me, a *Dharmatma* is firm in every action. It is not that I am just enunciating the Gita with firmness. I loved Radha with the same firmness! And know this well, Arjuna, that had I not immersed myself in my love for Radha with absolute firmness, today, I would neither have been able to enunciate the Gita with such conviction, nor would I have stood so firm in this battle of Mahabharata. Hence, bear in mind, Arjuna, that while absolute firmness mirrors the Soul, confusion is a proof of ego."

However, yet another point to understand here is that no human is born confused. All confusions in the human mind and heart have been created because of the teachings of duality spread by the so-called religions and the society. If you are wise, then take the hint as I have explained all that I could in brief. Just bear this in mind that you should try to finish as many tasks as you can with firmness. If you are able to complete a task or an action without worrying about its result, then do not worry about how the world would perceive your actions. Have faith in the firmness of the actions which naturally flow through you, and maintain firmness in every action you undertake. Eventually, there will come a day when your firmness will get the right direction from Nature. Many have received it, and so shall you. Therefore, kindly comprehend this science of firmness in its depth; this is a profound psychology. The very meaning of firmness is absence of worry about the result. If you worry about the result, then you shall never be able to carry out any task with firmness. Truly speaking, the psychological meaning of the statement, 'Just perform your actions and do not be worried about its result' is, every action must be performed with absolute firmness.

E) Express yourself completely

The life of a seeker is like an open book. They never try to hide anything either about themselves or about their actions out of fear of so-called religions, society, family, teachings or beliefs. Neither did Mahavira hide his nudity, nor did Bill Gates hide his atheism...they didn't need to! Those who are the 'decision-makers' and 'doers' of their actions, those who believe the system to be their own, or those who have allowed the so-called religions, society and beliefs to prevail over them, have a reason to hide. Look at Krishna! What all did he not do! But did he ever hide anything? Hence, only he who is true to himself, who expresses himself fully and portrays his actual self to the outside world, can be considered as living in close proximity to his Soul. And the one who hides everything about himself, thinking that his acts and thoughts can be negatively perceived by the world, is far from his Soul. Moreover, the person who puts on a facade of being someone he is not, can well be considered a person bereft of Soul. One must understand that there is nothing wrong with *Raasleela* or dancing with women. But yes, preaching against *Raasleela* in the day and engaging in the same at night is certainly not right. As they say, 'being a wolf in a sheep's clothing' is deception.

Thus, if you really wish to be closer to the powers of the Soul, then to an extent possible, portray your true self to the world and as far as possible, try not to bother about what people might have to say. This shall instantly strengthen your spiritual power. It does not matter 'who says what', what matters is, 'what you really are'! And you need to comprehend the scientific aspect behind it that when the system is not your own, then who are you to find faults in it and subsequently suppress it, or hide something about it? Those who believe, the system belongs to existence never indulge in such acts. They live in acceptance of the fact that no matter how they are, Nature has created them so, after due deliberation. Then what is there to hide? I just have to watch what the system created by Nature unfolds. Only he, who lives with such immense faith, can express himself fully as he really is. Indeed, this is the science behind expressing oneself fully.

In truth, the one who, instead of displaying superficial goodness, focusses on portraying his true self, will eventually move close to his Soul. It does not matter what kind of a person you are. What matters is, whether everyone is aware of the kind of person you are. If you are hiding your true self, then this masquerading will cost you dearly in several other aspects of life. And this too has a deep science of Nature embedded in it. Speaking in brief, as soon as a person hides or suppresses something, he digresses from the path of his destiny. And such people who have lost their path are called hypocrites. If you observe carefully, you will realise that this hypocrisy is proving detrimental for everyone in the world.

If you read the biography of any great person, you will find, as they led a life with sheer firmness, the world tried to find numerous vices in their lives; as this verily is the way of the world. And then, when they achieved great success, one day, the same world saluted them and sang their praises; this, again, is how the world operates. That is why, I am telling you, that it is only absolute honesty about your true self that can take you closer to your Soul. Do not resort to hypocrisy due to external pressures, influences and baseless beliefs. Otherwise, your life shall just flit by, without having gained anything worthwhile. Remember, there are deep secrets hidden in my statements. So, as long as hypocrisy exists within you, irrespective of what you do, you shall not be liberated.

F) The Soul just follows itself

I am giving you these tests, one after another, so as to enable you to gauge the level at which you stand with regard to your Soul, and know whether your Soul is awakened or dormant. And this is imperative as only the awakened Souls can carve a great life for themselves. Hence, I am giving you one more test to find out how awakened your Soul is. I shall try to explain you the scientific basis of this test by posing a question. Tell me; can the Soul, which is the omnipotent governing force of existence, follow anyone else? Just impossible! To follow others or to accord importance to others is the attribute of the system. For, it is oblivious of the great secret forces of Nature. But why would the Soul, in which all secret forces are interwoven, pay heed to anyone or anything that is in the external world? How would it matter to the Soul what someone else has to say? It would always play to its own tune!

Hence, if your actions are being influenced by what others have to say, then know that your Soul is not yet awakened. Because, how can the Soul, which is absolutely free and independent, be influenced by anything? Hence, take this as a scientific test; the more a person is affected by others' views and comments, the more distant he is from his Soul. Krishna is elucidating the same to Arjuna in the Gita. He says, "O Arjuna! The Soul follows its own self! Hence, if you wish to make a decision from your Soul, then you shall have to rise above scriptures and what is prescribed in them."

Do you want to become a historical legend? It is very easy... stop following others.

Let us delve a little deeper into this science! Soul is nothing but Nature! And Nature is creative, which means it is always engaged in creating something new. So, the closer one moves towards the Soul, the more he shall do something new, speak something new and live in his own novel way. And this is the very purpose of human life as well as the significance of realising the Soul. A human being has not come here to follow anyone, but to play his own novel, creative tune bestowed upon him by Nature. And the one who shields himself from the influence of others and starts to play his own tune, automatically begins to inch closer to his Soul. Thereupon, one day, he reaches so close to the Soul that

Nature's creativity flows through him. In other words, something unprecedented, that nobody has ever done before, stems forth from him. Then, it matters not which field that creativity takes place in—science, art, business or knowledge. This is the secret behind the great achievements of all eminent people.

In essence, the world is teeming with two kinds of people; first, those who follow others, and second, those who follow their own path. Those who follow others tend to increasingly overshadow their Souls by the day; and those who follow their own selves begin to inch closer to their Souls. And then one day, a miraculous creativity sent by Nature stems forth from such people who live by their own will, that is without being unnecessarily influenced by the outside world, and such miraculous creation earns them unprecedented greatness. Needless to say, the rest of the people just end up following in the footsteps of such great people through their life. Hence, wake up and realise that man has not come here to follow in someone's footsteps. Everyone has come into existence to play their own tune for the betterment of humanity.

To elucidate further, tell me, whom do you call Gods? It is those who sang their own tunes. Krishna did not repeat the Vedas and Upanishads. He sang his own new song in the form of the Bhagavad Gita. Buddha or Christ did not follow anyone, but sang their own new tune, in accordance with the prevalent time. Kabir also sang his own novel poems. In short, the one who is engaged in repetition is in a state of deep slumber. And the more one repeats, the deeper one shall slip into a slumber. One who learns the Gita by rote and repeats it shall surely go astray; but the one who adapts the Gita to the changing times shall be emancipated. However, as the world is replete with people who imitate others, humanity is in such a sorry state today. Funnily enough, the more a person imitates, the more religious he is considered, whereas at the level of true spiritual knowledge, he is nothing but a good parrot. It is not that the verses of Kabir were different in essence than the verses of the Gita! Essence was the same in both the cases, only the style of expression was adapted to the changing times. Truth is one, but it shall remain the truth only when it is adapted to the prevalent times.

In short, I have hinted towards the personality of the seeker, and how he lives his life. Now, you have to decide whether you wish to repeat the verses of Kabir or wish to let new verses spring forth from within? Know this as a rule that new original Mantras never stem forth from those who keep repeating old Mantras. Now, you have to decide whether you wish to continue reading how the Wright brothers invented the airplane or you wish to invent or discover something new yourself. If you wish to create something new, you shall have to get closer to your Soul. And if you wish to get closer to the Soul, you shall have to lead your life as Nature intended you to live i.e. live your life in your own way, think in your own novel manner and indulge in the actions of your choice. You shall have to safeguard your life from all external influences and surrender it to Nature. For, only then shall Nature be able to steer it according to its plan and make it a medium for what it wishes to accomplish. Know with certainty that whatever Nature wants to accomplish through you, would surely be nothing short of phenomenal.

Why do you not understand that it is not Nature but you who has created the differences of good-bad, sin-virtue and one's own-others'? That is why when Nature steers the system, it won't do so on the basis of such useless classifications or bondages. For Nature, everything is its own creation. Such being the case, against whom would it discriminate and why? Whom would it consider alien or bad, and why? I have given an indication of the 'free functioning' of Nature. Now, you yourself have to progress on this path and explore it further.

G) The Soul rejoices only in soulful emotions

No one desires to lead an unsuccessful life, and to that effect, everyone makes the best possible efforts. But the question

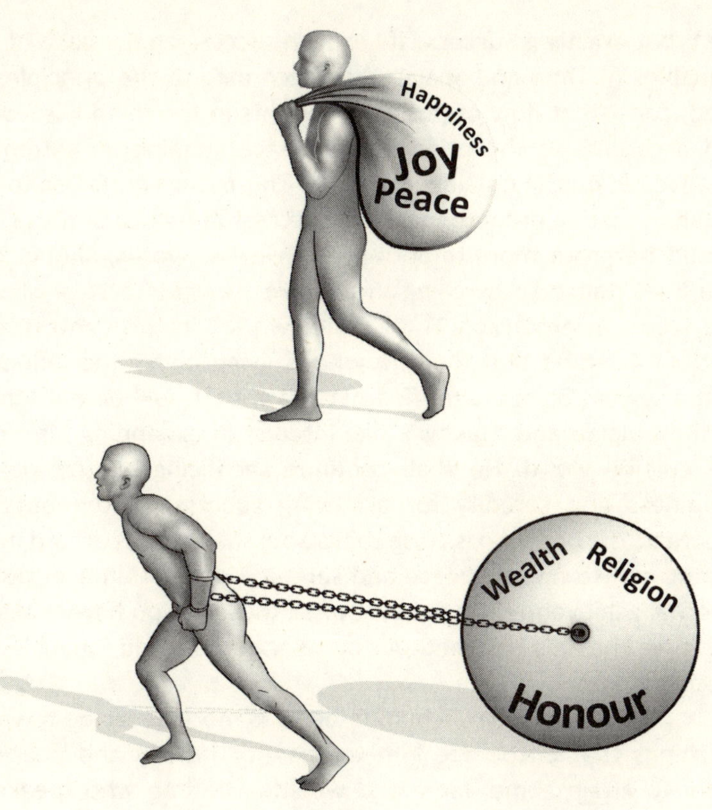

Who is Successful? Who is Unsuccessful?

It is the truth of life that all the successes
have been attained by those
who have been seekers of joy and peace.
Those who seek religion and wealth
and toil for the same have only found failure.

is – What exactly is success? If I explain success on the basis of the principles of Time and Space, then according to the principles of Time, consistent flow of positive thoughts in the mind is success, and according to the principles of Space, leading an extremely creative life on the outside is success. This in turn gives rise to the question that–in order to make life successful—which of these two should be given more importance? In other words, should one give importance to dwelling in positive thoughts first or should one focus on expansion in the outer world? In this context, one must understand that the one who is living under the influence of the system or has identified himself with it, will be enchanted by the outside and thus will take interest in expanding his life in the outside world. He shall continue sacrificing his joy, peace, happiness and serenity for achieving success on the outside. Whereas, the one who is close to his Soul shall always accord more importance to his joy, peace and serenity. He would never desire external achievement at the cost of all these. If you have realised, these are the only two methods popular in the world for achieving success in life!

Needless to say, a human being is more attracted towards teachings that encourage him to sacrifice his joy and peace in order to attain name, fame and wealth. The one who speaks of contentment is considered 'out of his mind' in this world. Ironically, even for the attainment of God and religion, human beings are being taught to sacrifice their joy and peace. But you must realise that all these teachings don't serve you in any way, and instead lead you astray. One can gain neither wealth nor religiousness through these methods. For ages, human beings have endeavoured to achieve success in the outside world by sacrificing their joy and peace thus. But how many have achieved a great life or self-realisation through these methods? Perhaps none! For, the truth of life is, all the successes have been attained by those who have been seekers of joy and peace and who refused to suffer for any attainment, even if it was wealth or religion. Also, history stands testimony to the fact that only those who have performed tasks for their own enjoyment have attained great success.

There lie many secrets behind this entire science. However, at present, you need to comprehend that the one, who is close to his Soul will not at all be entangled in this illusory world. Mansions, palaces and a sense of false honour are indeed a part of the illusory world, for, all these shall be left behind when the body perishes. The system might well be interested in all these, but not the Soul. The Soul needs and feeds only on those things that shall forever remain with oneself. And happiness, enjoyment and peace of mind are the experiences that eventually lead one to the powers which remain with a human being for many births to come. Hence, the one who is close to the Soul, shall be a seeker of only such beautiful feelings.

In a nutshell, grasp it once and for all that the one who has set out on the path of seeking joy and peace shall continue to move closer to his Soul. And one day, the powers of Nature shall do something phenomenally great in the life of the person who has reached closer to the Soul. Overnight, he shall surpass all humans who are making incessant efforts to achieve success in the outer world. From my end, I have given you an indication for progressing in the right direction. Now, it is your duty to break free of the trap of material needs and anchor yourself in spiritual needs. If you succeed, you will surely accomplish great feats, else, stuck in the grind, you shall continue to strive, in the hope of rising to glory. However, a point to ponder here is, how does it even matter if one does not acquire wealth and observe any religion? Just think, can any religion or wealth be greater than living life with joy, peace and happiness?! If you have still not been able to comprehend, then know for sure, that henceforth, even God will not be able to help you.

Spiritual Tests Have No Exceptions

There can be nothing wrong in the actions of the person with an awakened consciousness, and tasks executed by a slumbering consciousness are not acceptable to the Supreme Soul. Hence, when it comes to action, 'who is doing it' gains precedence over 'what one is doing'.

From my end, I have revealed seven tests or parameters to gauge one's closeness or distance from the Soul. Remember, these tests have been given to know the Soul. They are not some superficial, fictitious or baseless parameters from which one can draw numerous interpretations or exceptions. This is science! And science itself signifies that it is applicable without exception. If water evaporates when heated, then it would evaporate not only on earth, but also on Moon and Mars. It would evaporate not just in a temple or mosque, but even at home or in a pub. This is not a phenomenon that would discriminate and differentiate between places and mend its laws (for some). It is a pure science in which every place is just a place, without the distinction of 'good-bad' or 'yours-mine'.

So, the tests that I have listed to gauge one's closeness or distance from the Soul are totally based on the science of Nature; hence there are no exceptions to it. If pride is a proof of distance from the Soul, then it is! One cannot discriminate and construe pride for one's educational achievements as bad or pride for one's religion as good. No! In both cases, pride is equally bad and dangerous. So, please be kind enough not to interpret it any differently and look for any exceptions in the seven tests I have given, or you shall go astray. If attachment is bad, then it is bad whether it is for oneself, one's child, one's religion or even for God. Know with certainty that the problem is with attachment, not with the child or God.

All in all, only when you test yourself with such precision, shall you be able to assess yourself accurately. And only if you are able to assess yourself correctly, shall you be able to progress in the right direction. And only once you progress in the right direction, shall you be able to lead your life on the path to becoming great. Else, if you measure yourself on the basis of discriminations and exceptions, then you shall feel pleased and pompous for no rhyme or reason and harbour a delusory pride of being a good person. However, life is made not by basking in credulity, but by actually moving closer to the Soul. The statements I have made here are not religious teachings where you can burgle a house during the day and in the night, you can atone for the sin by visiting a temple, mosque or church. This is not a baseless science where after committing a sin, everything can be set right by taking a dip in the Ganges. This is a true science and you shall benefit from it only if you perceive it thus.

As I have already delved so deep into this discussion, I would like to state the last but significant point. The truth is, though humans have drawn an extensive list of sin-virtue and good-bad as per their understanding, it does not stop or prohibit people from indulging in wrong acts. Often, it has been observed that, people easily indulge in sinful acts in the name of virtue, and intentionally or unintentionally, they indulge in more wrongdoing under the delusion of virtuous acts. And all this shall persist as long as a human continues to live believing the system as his own. Because till a human considers the system as his own, he shall make efforts to protect it as well as to enhance and embellish it. And no one here has any idea about the extent of wrong deeds one performs while making these efforts.

I wonder, why do you not grasp the plain and simple science behind this: that as long as selfishness prevails among humans, they shall continue to harm numerous others in order to fulfill their selfish interests. And to harm others is the only sin. Only the one who stops considering the system as one's own can become free of this tendency. Unless this translates into reality, all teachings shall only prove to be banal and fictitious. For, a human shall be governed by Nature only when he stops considering the system as his own. And there is no question of a wrong deed happening in or through Nature. Whether your parochial thinking and short-sightedness fathoms this or not, the truth is, there can never be anything wrong in the final outcome of actions flowing forth from Nature. Hence, keep in mind not to decide 'what is good or bad' on the basis of the act or action per se. The righteousness of an act can only be determined by 'who' has done it and not by 'what' has been done. In other words, Krishna's or Buddha's actions could never translate into any wrongdoing irrespective of the nature of their actions; because they were not living their life considering the system as their own. After all, when one doesn't consider the system as one's own, how can anything wrong happen? Because, in such cases, when one doesn't consider the system as one's own, it will be governed by Nature. On the other hand, those who are firmly living under the misconception of considering the system as their own, will never be instrumental in doing anything right, irrespective of what they do. For, the root cause of all human evils is selfishness. If you awaken this awareness, this awareness alone will help you break free of many delusions. Then you shall not mislead yourself by finding exceptions in everything. Then you shall comprehend that pride per se is wrong, no matter what. Then it does not matter whether it is for a car or for a religion.

The Soul is a Mirror

Honesty is the greatest virtue of a human being.
And what is honesty?
To encapsulate it in a sentence,
being absolutely open and vocal about yourself,
about who you are and what is on your mind,
is the greatest honesty. Reread the biography
of all the successful and great people,
you will realise it.

The configuration of the Soul is such that it is well aware of everything as it is only a witness. Hence, whether it is the phenomena of Nature or the play of human life, Soul knows it all. That is why the wise savants say, a human need not learn anything, rather he only needs to awaken. For, as soon as one is awakened, the entire wisdom of Nature automatically kindles in him. This is the reason, why all the true teachings endeavour to awaken a human being rather than teach him.

Well, presently, rather than the play of Nature, we shall focus on the games human beings play, because a human is a few steps ahead of Nature in playing all sorts of games. He never reveals what he actually is. But he does not realise that he does not stand to gain anything by playing games. Because a human being may hoodwink the world by acting, hiding, pretending or claiming to be what he is not, but he cannot mislead the Soul. The Soul that dwells within him, is never deluded; the Soul is well aware of the truth and reality behind everything. When any person wrongs someone or speaks a lie, the Soul immediately makes him aware of his misdeeds and unfailingly it does; but when does a human, who is always worried about his system, ever pay heed to his Soul? He continues to indulge in all sorts of vices and covers them under the shroud of tall, egoistic claims.

Nevertheless, you need to forget about everyone else and think about yourself! You must understand that when your Soul becomes aware of all your actions – whether mental or physical, then what is the use of hiding them from the world? If you have harmed someone, then go and tell him, "Look brother! I have harmed you with a wrong intention." For, what is known to your Soul should be known to the other person as well. This one bit of honesty shall instantly take you closer to your Soul. So, from today onwards, decide once and for all, that whatever your Soul knows about you, must be known to everyone else too. Thereafter, you should not be bothered about the consequences. If you are affected by the consequences, you shall never be able to practise such honesty. 'It is easier said than done' is an apt expression for the message of the Gita, 'Perform your actions but do not worry about its result!' However, if you wish to lead your life truthfully, then boost your courage, show firmness, display honesty and respect Nature's creation. Indeed, when the magnificence of Nature's creation is such that nothing remains hidden from your Soul, then it behoves you to not try and hide anything. There lie great secrets hidden behind each creation of Nature. And you shall be able to

When can You Realise Your True Self

You have come into this world
to become who you are.
And you can become that
only if you are not influenced by external forces.

progress only by living in accordance with them. So, unless you are able to relinquish the desire for the result of your action, you shall not be able to garner such courage.

In essence, you shall have to be honest with yourself and stop worrying about the outcome for the sake of your own progress. Hence, decide that whatever is known to your Soul must be known to everyone else, too. Trust me, this bit of honesty alone shall bring about such a miraculous change in your life that you cannot even imagine. For, in doing so, you will fall in sync with all the powers of Nature. Nevertheless, I know that it is very easy to visit religious places but very difficult to live with such honesty. This is the reason why the number of people visiting a temple-mosque-church is approximately five hundred million, whereas the number of people living honestly is barely one or two million. However, the reality of life is, it is only these one-two million people who are truly more successful and prosperous than the rest.

Therefore, I shall once again state that stop worrying about the world and be as honest as you can. This one bit of respect for your Soul shall drastically change your life and lead you on the path to achieve greatness. The world will be left behind cursing you for your honesty, while you shall march ahead on the path of progress. Hence, do not resort to hypocrisy, for the sake of garnering respect from the outer world, otherwise, you shall be stuck in the grind. Always remember that even if the entire world becomes your enemy, you must still maintain harmony with your Soul. For, eventually, a day will come when the world will be left bewildered; it will watch you in amazement and will be compelled to respect you and acknowledge your worth. Indeed, it would be interesting to see how many people can muster the courage to live with such honesty!

Recognise People Living in Spiritual Totality

*The wise ones
are not internally affected
by 'external matters'.*

Apparently, the world is teeming with wise people and Gods. But how would you measure them on the parameters of Soul and gauge, how many of them are actually living by the Soul and how many by the ego? In this regard, one must comprehend a few points listed here. The Soul is absolutely free and creative. In other words, a seeker shall neither copy anyone nor follow anyone. He shall not be bound by any worldly bondage. Also, as he is a pure Soul and not the system, he will be devoid of all kinds of selfish instincts. There shall be absolute firmness in his actions. Even if the entire world is against him, it cannot deviate him from the path of his actions or change his course. And as he is not the system but the Soul, he is concerned not about his system but the betterment of the entire world. Thus, I have briefly stated the signs of a seeker.

Here, I am throwing light on these attributes because there is no dearth of supposedly wise people and so-called Gods, but it is important to know how many among them are actually gods and wise. There have been many who have gone unsung in the annals of history, or who at present are not revered as part of history, but were actually supremely wise. At the same time, there are many who are being worshipped today, when in fact, they were worse than ordinary human beings. My intention here is to just convey the signs of truly wise people, for you to identify them so that you can benefit from their knowledge and lives. And with that, I also wish that you stop going astray by wrongly believing some people to be wise or gods.

Let me elaborate this by citing the examples of Christ, Meera and Socrates and introduce you to the power of their Soul. I am sure, with the help of these three examples, you shall glean the true essence and inner strength of people aligned with their Soul. Consequently, you shall surely be spared of worshipping falsely presumed gods and imbibing knowledge from ignorant people. This is indeed imperative, in order to steer life in the right direction. Hence, without further ado, let us delve into the inner strength of people anchored in the Soul with the examples of Christ, Meera and Socrates.

Inner Strength of Christ

*When you are awakened,
you will not desire the result of your action.
Instead, you will decide the outcome.*

Is there anyone who does not know about Jesus Christ? I guess not! Hence, I shall just highlight the power of his Soul in brief. As you know, Christ was born in a Jewish family. Perhaps, you have only come across people who follow the ancestral religion of the family, and take pride in it. Amusingly, the world is teeming with such people, but this is a sign of a dormant Soul. An awakened Soul is not confined to the dictates of religion, society, caste and country; he breaks free of them in an instant and marches ahead. Surpassing all barriers, he embraces one and all with equal love and affection. Christ, an awakened Soul that he was, followed the same course; he opened his arms for one and all beyond race, religion and nationality. Going a step further, he not only defied Judaism, but also set out to vehemently protest against prevalent hypocrisies. Here, understand that – Can he, who worries about his system ever oppose Jewish hypocrisies on a Jewish land, where the entire population comprises Jews, and that too, orthodox, fanatical Jews? No way! He shall panic at the very thought of it! However, Christ was nothing but a pure Soul! And why would the Soul worry about what happens to the system?

Fervidly, Christ began to speak against the Jewish hypocrisies prevalent in those times. As it was expected, he faced strong opposition and his system was threatened. For, the fanatical Jews were obviously not able to tolerate Christ's attacks on their hypocrisies for long. And at last, these fanatical Jews captured Christ, while he was resting on a mountain, and produced him in a court of law. However, there was no question of Christ, who stood resolute in his spiritual firmness, reneging on his beliefs, statements or actions; even so, they tried their best to dissuade him. In fact, when their tactic failed, they even threatened him as best as they could. This is because every propagator of fanaticism aims to make the detractors surrender by hook or by crook. But all their efforts, be it dissuasion or threats, made no dent on Christ's psyche, which was fortified with the strength of the Soul. Only those who have identified themselves with the system worry about negative consequences, not Christ.

In the end, the ignorant bunch of religious fanatics did what they could do best. Christ was sentenced to crucifixion. And crucifixion is no easy death! While at gallows, sharp nails were continuously pierced into his body until the very life force departed from his body. But what difference was this going to make to Christ who was throbbing with the immense power of the Soul! He wore a beatific smile on his face even while being led to his crucifixion. On the other hand, the religious fanatics displayed their inhuman side by pounding nails into different parts of Christ's body. Blood began to spurt from each pierced part of his body. But the smile on Christ's lips still did not wane. In the end, he breathed his last with these words on his lips—'Oh Lord! Forgive them, for, they know not what they are doing!'

Now, there lie several profound meanings hidden in this one sentence uttered by Christ. Firstly, what he is saying is, these ignorant people are punishing my system, whereas the entire play is of my Soul. Hence, O Lord, forgive this folly on their part. Secondly, these people are of the thinking that the death of Christ's body spells the death of Christ. Now who can make these ignoramuses understand that Christ is not a body at all? Christ is a Soul that was always there, always is and shall always be. Thirdly, these ignoramuses are rejoicing and revelling for, they believe they have captured Christ and crucified him. They fail to realise that crucifixion was my own choice. I well knew that a few strong words spoken against these fanatical Jews will lead these people to resort to this mindless act. And verily, this foolish act on their part will trigger a rippling effect, which will rapidly spread my teachings far and wide across the world. Else, even if I spend my entire life striving to make each person see reason, I shall not be able to fulfill my purpose in this world. Also, O Lord, please forgive them for nurturing such false pride.... In short, it was this power of Soul, inner strength, spiritual wisdom and far-sightedness of Christ that made him omnipresent in this whole world.

Nevertheless, you all need to introspect a little. First of all, you barely do anything noble for anyone, and even when you do, you inevitably expect something in return. And if by mistake, the beneficiary of your noble deed does not recognise your nobleness or feel obliged towards you, then it enrages you. On the other hand, Christ did everything for the betterment of humanity; but what did he get in return? An extremely brutal and excruciatingly painful death! Even so, did you even hear a murmur of complaint? Did the thought ever cross his mind that, "Despite working for the betterment of these people, what did I receive in return? Crucifixion?" No! Seekers of the Soul never think thus. They are simply concerned with the thorough execution of their task and firmness of their action. For them, the outcome of the task is nothing more than a show to watch.

In all, I have given you a glimpse of 'Christ's Soul' in its totality. Henceforth, read and listen to only those who have the power of Soul, inner strength, spiritual thinking, firmness and selflessness similar to that of Christ's. Moreover, please note, even if mistakenly you pay heed, and try to understand or worship egoists, believing them to be the upholders of spiritual knowledge, then you will be trapped. I am sure you are wise enough to take the hint!

Inner Strength of Meera

A child's mind is akin to a blank slate. Therefore, before advising them or giving them a present, always think a thousand times.

Meera, an embodiment of love, needs no introduction. Perhaps, there is hardly anyone in India who is oblivious to Meera's life; but now the time has come for the entire world to recognise her greatness. Emphatically, in order to make it easier for everyone to comprehend, I shall provide you a glimpse of the power of her Soul. Meera was born in a royal household, where all her family members were devotees of Krishna. When she was barely 4-5 years old, her family began to narrate stories of Krishna to her. Her mind was a blank slate on which the enchanting tales of Krishna were leaving an indelible mark. As a result, it was but natural for her to develop feelings for Krishna. Oftentimes in jest, her family even stated that Krishna was her husband and such statements inevitably left an imprint on her mind. And at this juncture, it is imperative to comprehend the psyche of a child. Their minds are blank, not cluttered with useless thoughts and ideologies. Hence, many statements tend to take root very deep into their minds. It is, therefore, crucial to be very careful while communicating with children. We shall discuss this in detail when I speak on child psychology. At present, grasp it well that on the one hand, there was Krishna's charming persona, and on the other, the impressionable mind of little Meera. Consequently, Meera, in sheer innocence, completely believed the statement 'Krishna was her husband' to be true and allowed it to take root deep into her Soul.

With the passage of time, Meera grew up to be a young and beautiful girl. But even when she had grown up, the attraction she had for Krishna showed no signs of abating. On the contrary, it was growing stronger as the years elapsed. This was the reason why she was never interested in the ostentatious flamboyance of the royal family, and rather preferred to spend time with herself. And with the passage of time, she began to enjoy her solitude. She would always remain lost in her own world. However, no one took her love for solitude very seriously. They certainly attempted to coax her to be more sociable, but would then leave it at that, believing it to be just a trait of her personality.

Gradually, Meera attained puberty, and then one day, the tide of time turned. As was the tradition of the royal families, Meera was married off to a prince–Rana Bhoj, the prince of Mewar. Although Meera was not at all excited about her marriage, she quietly acquiesced to it, relenting to the demands of the family. So far, everything moved smoothly, but the situation changed dramatically when, on her wedding night, she shocked Rana with her proclamation that she was already married to Krishna and belonged only to him! In other words, Meera's love for solitude was rooted in her love for Krishna. On the other hand, no one ever realised that what was spoken in jest would, in fact, leave an indelible mark on Meera's mind and grow to such humongous proportions.

Life is all about Joy

To live a joyful life free of worries is the only purpose of human life.

But it had! Fortunately, Rana was a gentle and sensible man. Even though he was shocked by Meera's statement, and taken aback at her resoluteness, he maintained his composure, conducted himself in a courteous manner and let sensibility prevail. However, he was still at a loss of words on how to reason with her. As a matter of fact, Krishna had lived thousands of years ago, so his dilemma was, how should he construe Meera's proclamation of being married to Krishna? How much importance should he accord to it? While Rana was caught in a dilemma, Meera, on her part, was absolutely clear that she belonged only to Krishna.

Thus, at the end, in view of Meera's firmness and her innocence, Rana decided to leave her alone for some time. Well, this was the greatness of Rana, but on the other hand, he also had family members to deal with, especially, his father, the King. And since the King was very disciplined and strict by nature, it was out of question for him to accept the situation. He pressurised Rana Bhoj to persuade Meera, and if need be, to use harsh words. But Rana was not in favour of using harsh language. On the contrary, he had fallen for Meera's firm and innocent demeanour. At the same time, Meera's obsession with Krishna was on the rise with each passing day. And Rana did not wish to become an obstacle in this innocent love of Meera. But how could his family remain silent and for how long? Besides, the royal family became all the more perturbed when news of Meera's love for Krishna spread like wildfire. Everyone was amused for, their princess was in love with Krishna, who had bid adieu to this world thousands of years ago. Krishna, who existed 5000 years ago, is the husband of our new princess?! Since the news was certainly stupefying in nature, it immediately caught people's fancy and spread far and wide.

On the other hand, Meera was also very firm. It was not in her nature to keep matters of the heart a secret. By way of her words and behaviour, she continued to leave an impression on people that she was Krishna's wife. It was natural then, for tongues to wag! But, for how long could the royal family tolerate all this? So,

Rana's father and other family members pressurised him further to control Meera, even though Rana was a man who preferred counselling and reasoning instead of pressurising. It was indeed a Herculean task to make an adamant Meera, who was completely besotted by Krishna, see reason.

In short, Rana was perturbed, his family suffered the ignominy of Meera's behaviour and the King was beside himself with fury. As the situation was turning from bad to worse with each passing day, Rana's father and the royal priest decided to take matters in their hands and launched a two-pronged attack on Meera by exerting emotional pressure on her. Rana was not at all pleased with this, but there was not much he could do in the face of the King's obstinate stance! However, their pressure tactics had an altogether reverse effect on Meera. Instead of succumbing to their pressure, Meera became even more resolute and her inner strength that had its source in Krishna's form, manifested itself even more strongly. She even admitted in the royal court that Krishna was her husband, and vehemently criticised the royal priest in the court for his hypocritic religious practices. She also vociferously protested against animal sacrifice. In other words, riding high on her passion for Krishna, Meera's spiritual power was growing by leaps and bounds, and it grew to such an extent that it turned Meera into a poet. Poetry laden with her love for Krishna stemmed from deep within her; and she penned several Soul-stirring poems, each one surpassing the other. In other words, because of her love for Krishna, the wisdom and the artistic talent of Krishna began to flow forth from her. This too is Nature's own science. We shall discuss this science in detail, while discussing the science of frequency. Presently, you just need to understand that if you instate someone deep in your heart, gradually, you tend to become exactly like them. Hence, it would be prudent to give considerable thought before according a prominent place to someone in your heart.

Nevertheless, how could the ego of the royal family digest such honest statements of Meera? Indubitably, aggrieved and agitated, the royal court's attitude turned harsh towards her. However, their behaviour had little effect on Meera who had completely assimilated Krishna in her Soul. Nestling Krishna in her heart, she took to the streets singing and dancing, extolling her love for him. And then she danced with abandon, so much so that she has been immortalised in the annals of history! Now how would the royal family tolerate the honourable princess of their palace dancing on the streets? Well, this was the problem of the royal family! On the other hand, how could even the common folk, approve the idea of a married woman, and that too, their princess—the wife of their beloved prince—dancing on the streets? But why would Meera be bothered with all this? For, this was the problem of people with a parochial mindset. With Krishna dwelling in her heart, Meera swayed with such elation that nothing else mattered to her! Everyone was confounded with such a bold and blunt attitude of indifference on Meera's part. Because as per general perception, the circumstances were obviously turning from bad to worse for Meera. On the one hand, the common folk were harassing Meera, and on the other, the pressure mounted by the royal court was also at its peak. In other words, on the one hand, the common people were pelting stones at Meera, and on the other, the royal soldiers were leaving no stone unturned in their attempts to harass Meera. But Meera's love for Krishna was so overpowering that with every bit of harassment, her bliss and joy were scaling new heights.

Indeed, the one who basks in spiritual joy becomes impervious to the torture and travails of the outside world. Unaffected by the stones being pelted at her and the abuses being hurled, Meera danced on the streets revelling in her spiritual joy. Needless to say, her evergrowing joy only fanned the fury raging in everyone's heart. Well, so be it! How did it matter to Meera? Just imagine her state of exuberance, stemming from the power of her Soul, that she even rejoiced in the stones pelted at her! Here, let me make it clear that one should not believe in fictitious tales and think that the miraculous power of Krishna turned the stones pelted at her into flowers. Remember, no such thing is possible as Nature functions according to its set laws. But of course, the human Soul, in its immense capacity, indeed, has the power to feel the fragrance and softness of flowers even in the stones thrown at oneself.

Nevertheless, as the scale of harassment increased, so did Meera's exuberance. On the other hand, the ego of the royal court, the common people and the self-professed caretakers of religion and society was finding it intolerable to bear the ignominy of this bitter defeat. So, as is the norm, the egoists began to display their cruelty. For, on one hand, it was beyond the tolerance of the royal court to watch their honourable princess dance on the streets, and on the other, the caretakers of religion and society were greatly offended by their defeat. Consequently, their joint nexus pronounced Meera a culprit and produced her before the royal court. Several charges were levelled against her. She was also threatened with dangerous punishments on the basis of those charges. But all this failed to produce any effect on Meera, and this certainly was a great defeat for their ego. For, when someone does not surrender to pressure tactics, the ego is bound to get hurt. However, the ego is very clever too as it is adept at changing colours like a chameleon. This is exactly what the king and the royal priest did! When fear failed to find its mark, they deployed greed as their weapon to weaken her. Both of them assured Meera that if she agreed to relinquish her love for Krishna, then she could once again enjoy a splendorous life in the royal palace, and all her past sins would be forgiven.

Ordinarily, such weapons in the form of fear and greed deployed by rulers and priests can surely enslave the common people, but how could these worthless weapons influence a person like Meera, who was brimming with the power of her Soul?! At the same time, perturbed by the ongoing drama, Rana Bhoj too tried his best to counsel Meera. Although Meera had great respect for him in her heart, she could not accept his advice. This was Nature's plan for Meera! So, neither did she accept, nor did she surrender. On the contrary, at every instance, she continued to fiercely attack the royal priest. In a way, she narrated the entire Gita to him. The royal priest, without a doubt, was left speechless, hearing the truth pouring forth from Meera. Indeed, how could a religious bigot succeed before a spiritually enlightened Meera? But, does the ego ever have any interest in the truth? If it did have, would it not have commended Christ instead of crucifying him? But it would not be 'ego' if it ever sided with the truth. Ego is interested only in making others bow down to its command. And in case someone does not bow down, it resorts to oppression. And that is exactly what happened here as well! When Meera did not buckle under their pressure, she was sentenced to death by poison!

Unfortunately, the self-professed caretakers and followers of religion have been adhering to such practices for ages! This habit of the societal guardians is centuries old. Indeed, their very nature is to suppress and harass every person who instead of following them, abides by the truth. Just look at the inner strength, truthfulness and honesty of Meera! When Krishna was ensconced in her heart and being; she did not hide it, instead she fully expressed it. Nothing mattered to her, be it family, husband, society, religion or people! To her, all were plain lies; only the Krishna dwelling in her heart was the truth! This is the truth of the Soul, and the firmness which stems from it refuses to prostrate before any power or pressure of useless dogmas, beliefs and bondages. I truly commend and salute Meera's inner strength which she drew from her love for Krishna and which transformed an ordinary woman like her into a great poetess, infusing her heart with the ultimate heights of knowledge and the science of religion.

Is Death a Reality?

Once you have realised your Soul,
you must stay awakened.
Then why compromise for anything?

To understand whether death is a reality, I shall now give you an example which will enable you to thoroughly grasp the ultimate influence of the Soul and will help you imbibe the fearlessness and the courageousness of the Soul. You must have heard the name of Socrates, a pivotal and enigmatic figure in Greek philosophy.

The great philosopher, Socrates was an extremely wise man, and always pertinent when expressing his views; his words inevitably carried a profound meaning. Socrates was fond of holding long discussions and debates on myriad topics and loved to counsel people. But as his words always bore the ring of truth, it was not surprising that his opinions and ideas often went against the prevalent, false societal beliefs, popular in his time. And as it did, he drew the ire of not only the common man, but also of the local administration. He was warned to refrain from uttering anything that was considered offensive, against the prevalent norms of the society. But the incorrigible Socrates continued to raise their hackles at every opportunity.

Finally, left with no other option, the administration had to arrest Socrates and produce him in court for trial. Since everyone was keen to see the outspoken and insolent Socrates in the dock, a large number of people gathered in court to witness the trial. As the trial began, a list of transgressions committed by Socrates was read out by the prosecutors, accusing him of instigating common citizens against popular customs, beliefs and social norms, by using insistence and coercion. Hearing this, the judge, who was a conservative and staunch follower of the prevalent traditions was livid with rage. Familiar with Socrates' antics, he already bore a grudge against him. Unleashing his fury at Socrates, he thundered, "Do you plead guilty to these charges?"

Socrates simply laughed and replied, "Yes, Your Honour."

Taken aback at this reply, the judge spoke to him in a grave tone, "Alright then, forgetting whatever has happened so far, if you can convince the court that you will reform your ways, the jury might consider showing you some mercy."

But Socrates was incorrigible. His sole purpose in life was to dispel the darkness of ignorance prevalent among people and to help them see the light of truth. So, he humbly replied to the judge, "Sorry, Your Honour, but I don't think I can mend my ways."

No sooner did the judge hear this audacious reply, than his face turned livid with rage. Even so, struggling to control his fury, he glowered at Socrates, and spoke in a menacing tone, "Think it over; because if you do not give this assurance, then I shall pronounce the death sentence upon you."

Without hesitating even for a moment, Socrates immediately retorted, "What is there to think about, Your Honour? I am definitely not going to change my ways. You are free to use your discretion and sentence me as you deem fit."

On hearing this, the infuriated judge immediately ordered that Socrates be put to death by making him drink poison. As soon as the sentence was pronounced, Socrates was chained and imprisoned. Barring a few of his disciples and well-wishers, everyone hailed the verdict and a jubilant mood pervaded the atmosphere.

On the other hand, a pall of gloom had descended over Socrates' disciples. Still, acting to the best of their understanding, to raise Socrates' spirits against the jubilation of people, they began visiting him regularly in prison. However, Socrates was absolutely unaffected by the death sentence. On the contrary, he consoled everyone, saying, "Oh fellows! Why are you so sad? Administering poison is in their hands, but to die or not is entirely up to me! So, do not worry. I will not die, even when the poison is administered!"

Though Socrates' words failed to kindle a feeling of reassurance in his disciples, they knew that arguing with their master would be a futile exercise. Besides, Socrates' cheerful attitude despite the death sentence, compelled them to believe in the possibility of his survival. Several days elapsed, in this ambiguous manner, and finally the day of Socrates' execution arrived. Many of his disciples gathered close to him in his final hour, some weeping copiously. But in stark contrast to all of them, Socrates was brimming with exuberance; there was no trace of fear or anxiety either on his face or in his behaviour. On the contrary, he was eagerly waiting for the poison to be administered to him. He was sure that the poison would have no effect on him! Meanwhile, even the man concocting the hemlock (a poisonous European plant), was stunned to see Socrates' cheerful demeanour. He was also clearly upset, for, his poison would put such a cheerful man to death. He knew that he could not save Socrates, but yes, he could at least delay his death as much as possible; thinking thus, the man took his time to prepare the hemlock. Clearly, his intention was to let Socrates live as much as he could. But Socrates was astute; he had gauged the intention of the man concocting the poison. Eagerly waiting, Socrates soon became impatient and told the man, "Why are you wasting time?

And why are you looking so despondent? You are not administering the poison to me; it is the blind followers of tradition who are doing so. You are merely discharging your duty. Hence, perform your duty with utmost sincerity and quickly administer the poison to me."

With a heavy heart, the man prepared the poison and administered it to Socrates. The poison quickly spread in the body and its effect could clearly be seen by one and all. As soon as it affected his feet, they became numb, but Socrates was not one to be affected. Instead, he told his disciples in his inimitable style, "My feet have become numb, but I am still alive!" Meanwhile, the hemlock had spread to his arms and abdomen. Describing his condition to the disciples, Socrates spoke again, "The poison has now consumed seventy per cent of my body... but I am still alive." Finally, when the hemlock spread to his brain and heart, the entire body was affected; even so, in a soft whisper, Socrates murmured, "Listen, O people of the world! The poison has almost destroyed my entire body! But I am still alive. This means, there is no greater unreality than death." With these words on his lips, Socrates breathed his last, but became immortal in the history of mankind.

Indeed, this is not only Socrates' story, but the story of the immortality of every Soul. Each one of us here was, is and will always be the eternal Soul. And irrespective of what happens, the Soul has nothing to lose or gain. Simply stated, the one who realises this eternal truth, will be able to live his life with joyous abandon. But the one who has identified himself with the system instead of the Soul, will never be able to do what Socrates did. Such a person will neither be able to raise his voice against prevalent beliefs and traditions, nor will he be able to put his 'system' at stake in the interest of the greater good. Therefore, you shall have to imbibe the truth propounded by Socrates and marshal the courage to stand with the truth. Only then you shall be able to stand apart from the milieu and accomplish innovative and great feats. However, for the present, you must derive an understanding from the truth established by Socrates that a person who lives his life on the strength of his Soul shall never bow down to futile and false beliefs or traditions. Needless to say, the one who doesn't bow down to anyone or anything that is wrong, would surrender himself to Nature and accomplish unprecedented grand feats in life.

Now, just feel this inner strength within and check whether there exists even an iota of such strength in you. If it does not exist, then understand that your Soul is in a dormant state. Those who are reeling under the influence of innumerable bondages and pressures should consider themselves in a deep slumber at the spiritual level. When the Soul is the ultimate power in this universe, before whom would it bow down and to whom would it listen? Whenever the Soul awakens in a person, it shall play to its own unique tune. Hence, as much as possible, try to inch closer to this power of the Soul. The closer you get to the power of your Soul, the more your fears shall be dispelled from within. And then, one day, the awakened powers of your Soul shall set an exemplary precedent before the world. I wish you all the best for setting a great example powered by your inner strength and the power of your Soul.

One Cannot Progress Without Inching Closer to the Soul

The Soul is not at all concerned with external circumstances. The world is full of people who remain joyous in the worst circumstances as well as those who crib and cry despite having everything in life.

Our discussion so far has given us a better understanding of everything with reference to the Soul. With the examples of Christ, Meera and Socrates, we have also realised the supreme authority of the Soul. However, many of you may still be wondering why should we burden ourselves with an additional task of inching closer to the Soul, especially in today's busy and fast-paced world? You may well ask, what would happen if we don't inch closer to the Soul? If such questions are germinating in your mind, then you must know with certainty that you haven't thoroughly grasped the discussion so far. And if this is the case, then let me use a different approach to elucidate the point I want to drive home. For, inching closer to the Soul is of paramount importance to human life. In fact, the design of Nature is such, that it is not possible for one to progress or change one's life for the better without doing so. In fact, to inch closer to the Soul is the only duty one has, while the rest of it follows automatically. This is the reason why, in the oldest and most profound psychologies, the Soul holds paramount significance and is considered the supreme authority of existence. You don't have to move closer to your Soul to please the Almighty. No, not at all! You need to do it only because it is essential for the betterment of your life. For, the state of one's life is directly proportional to one's proximity to one's Soul. And as I don't leave a topic unexplained after broaching it, let me explain the significance of the Soul with a scientific approach, and with proof. And to this effect, you must first grasp that your life and world is divided into four layers.

Soul

The Soul can be termed as your innermost layer, which is the real 'you'! One who does nothing, but only watches. The very play of this Soul or this supreme void is such that despite doing nothing, it is the only one doing everything! Although the Soul is a mere spectator, without its presence, everything goes haywire and all your efforts come to naught. But how? Well, it is because your three powerful minds are very close to this profound layer—the Soul, and one cannot progress or change for the better without activating these three powerful minds. To explain this in depth, I shall shed light on these powerful minds and their influences.

Powerful Minds

Success, be it of any kind, can only be achieved with the help of the powerful minds. And these powerful minds are the superconscious mind, the spontaneous mind and the collective

You are born free

Your mind, brain, ego, body, senses are different from who 'you' are. This realisation will liberate you this very moment.

conscious mind. Speaking of the superconscious mind, it is replete with qualities such as enthusiasm, determination, concentration, common sense, so on and so forth. Bereft of these qualities, one cannot even afford to think of achieving success. The second is the spontaneous mind, which is the most powerful processor a human being has, and it works a million times faster than the brain. It is capable of producing a result by doing the most complex calculations in a fraction of a second. And the third is the collective conscious mind, which is connected with the consciousness of all human beings and can gauge other people's minds in the blink of an eye. And you must know that it is from this mind that all creativity flows forth. Hopefully, by now, you must have realised that success can only be achieved with the help of these three minds, and nothing else. And only those who are close to their Soul can comprehend the play of these minds. Indubitably, all the great people in the world fall in this category. With your limited understanding, you might assess great people on the basis of a particular ideology or belief, but in reality, all of them, without exception, are living close to their Soul. Needless to say, their success can be accredited to the superlative qualities of their powerful minds. Therefore, if you wish to progress in life or carve a great life for yourself, you have no other option but to inch closer to the Soul. For, these three minds can become active only once you are close to the Soul. And once these three minds are active, success will come knocking at your door. The power of these three minds will carve a special niche for you from the teeming millions and overnight, catapult you to the zenith of success. If you wish to comprehend the complete science of these powerful minds, read my book, '*I am The Mind*'.

Weaker Minds

If you are distant from the Soul, you will have no other option but to dwell in the weaker minds—conscious mind, sub-conscious mind and unconscious mind. The roots of all your negative emotions such as worries, frustration, sorrow, fear, etc.

lie in these minds. Hence, please do not erroneously assume that your life is full of perils, and so, you are gripped by worries, fears and insecurities. No...you are only bearing the repercussion of being distant from the Soul. But what can one do if there is a dearth of psychological knowledge in this regard? Well, before we answer that, I would like you to answer my question; aren't many people living in a condition far worse than yours, leading a joyous life? Doesn't history bear testimony to the lives of free-spirited fakirs (paupers) who have led their lives with unbridled joy and contentment? For a better comprehension of this point, you need not go far; you have just had a glimpse of the lives of Christ, Socrates and Meera in this book. Hence, instead of being swayed by baseless talks, you must bear in mind that without inching closer to the Soul, your pain, sorrows or fears are not going to dissipate. Unless you realise this truth, you will have to continue relying on your weak minds. But if you wish to lead a great life...sooner or later, you shall have to inch closer to the Soul; not to become Christ, Meera or Socrates, but to carve a better life for yourself.

The Soul can be termed as your innermost layer, which is the real 'you'! One who does nothing, but only watches.

Brain-Ego

If your distance from the Soul is greater, then caught in the delusion, you shall accord greater importance to your brain and ego. And since your weak minds are close to your brain-ego, whatever you shall do driven by your brain-ego, in the end, you shall always be gripped by fear, worries and sorrows. And as ninety-nine per cent of the people are distant from their Soul, they are all compelled to lead a sorrowful existence, for one reason or another. I hope, you must have now comprehended the significance of inching closer to the Soul. For a wise and sensible man, an indication is enough, so beware and become alert while there is still time. For, it is imperative for you to grasp that without inching closer to the Soul, life shall not change for the better. And since the very aim of true spirituality is to enhance one's life, all psychological texts accord prime importance to inching closer to the Soul.

Comprehend the Science of Self-realisation

Now, you need to comprehend that whether it is the Soul and the powerful minds, or, the weaker minds and the brain-ego, everything exists within you. And what is their role, you may ask? Only one – to establish your connection with the external world. Indeed, the entire play of your life depends on how well you perform in the external world. And you too evaluate everything including your fellow human beings on the same parameter. A person is exalted to the heights of greatness when he accomplishes great feats in the external world or is extolled for his fortune when he amasses wealth in the external world. In other words, the actions performed by a human being in the external world are well reflective of his inner state. Simply put, it is but the inner state of a human being that manifests outside. This also implies that if you want to scale the peaks of success in the external world, then you need to strengthen your inner self. Else, there is no method to achieve success directly on the outside. But, as everyone is hell-bent on carving a better or a great life with the help of external teachings and influences, they are unable to succeed. Only those who are wittingly or unwittingly inching closer to their Soul are able to make their life worthwhile. In the above-mentioned statements, I have briefly explained the complete science behind the successful life of a human being.

Now, you need to comprehend what exactly you are. Either you are the Soul and the powerful minds or you are the weaker minds and the brain-ego. Whoever you are and wherever you are, your connection with the external world is established from that point itself.

As ninety-nine per cent of the people dwell in the weaker minds and the brain-ego, they establish their connection with the outside world on the strength of these minds. For, this is the reason they create new problems for themselves time and again. At the same time, those who are close to the Soul, establish a connection with the outside world on the strength of their powerful minds; these are the people we know as Einstein, Ghalib, Kabir, Picasso, Newton, Bill Gates...and this is why self-realisation is imperative. Since you are living in the scientific age, I hope, you will instantly get the hint and set sailing for the wonderful journey called life...!

Simple Methods for Self-realisation

The sense of 'Me','Mine' and 'My own' is the only cause of worry. Try and worry without indulging in 'Me', 'Mine' and 'My own'; can you?

After the detailed discussion we have had so far, I hope you must have realised the importance of inching closer to the Soul. So, now, I shall straightaway expound upon a few solutions for realising your Self.

Break the delusion of 'Me', 'Mine' and 'My Own'

Have you ever pondered on this question: Why are you so distant from your own Soul? Simply because you have established your connection with the outside world on the basis of the brain-ego. Needless to say, the brain-ego are driven by attachment, i.e. they instantly assume everything as their own. Whereas, in truth, firmly assuming anything in the external world as one's own is a delusion; and this delusion creates a wide chasm which takes one further away from his Soul. When in fact, you are but the Soul. Even your body, with which you have identified yourself, has been given to you by Nature for only this lifetime. In that case, how can you assume materialistic possessions such as a house, car, wealth, etc. as your own? But you do, don't you? Consequently, you get stressed and your head begins to reel with the slightest up and down in any of them. And this very foolishness is termed as sorrow, pain, tension and fear. In other words, at the first stage, caught in this delusion, you assume that which is not 'yours', as your 'own'. Then on that basis, you unnecessarily inflate your notions of 'me', 'mine' and 'my own'. And no sooner you face a trouble with any 'me', 'mine' or 'my own', than you slip into the abyss of distress. But the question is, why do you indulge in such foolhardiness in the first place? The answer is, simply because you are far away from your Soul. Thus, if you want to rid yourself of these futile blows, then weaken your feelings of 'me', 'mine' and 'my own'.

In case you lose your wealth or your car meets with an accident, instead of grieving over it, sit in solitude with your eyes closed and repeat this affirmation, "It was never mine, so how can I lose it? I am but the Soul, and only 'that' which I have brought with me at the time of birth is 'mine'. Everything and everyone else are just fellow travellers who accompany me on this journey. They are bound to meet and part ways. Thus, I shall not mourn the loss of those who are meant to meet and part ways." This affirmation will instantly rid you of the delusion that the car was 'yours' and in an instant, the distance between you and your Soul shall reduce. And if the proximity with the Soul is maintained, your sorrows shall dissipate in no time and the power to buy ten more cars shall also remain intact.

Once you have successfully practised this experiment with objects, don't stop there. For, you are more ensnared by human beings than you are by objects. In other words, the delusion is deep-rooted and the journey is long. And with regards to human beings, your delusion of 'me', 'mine' and 'my own' is much stronger. But even in this case, everyone is meant to meet and part ways. Neither is anybody born with you, nor shall anyone follow you to your grave. Thus, whenever you are gripped by sorrows resulting from other people, immediately resort to this exercise; sit in solitude and affirm yourself, "I am nothing but the Soul. I am alone. Only that which I brought with me is 'mine'. Only 'that' which I shall take with me is 'mine'. The rest are just my fellow travellers; they shall meet and part ways. I only have to perform my duties towards them..." With this affirmation, you will instantly be freed of sorrows. And no sooner are you free of sorrows than your proximity to the Soul shall increase.

Follow the same practice even while dealing with the ailments of your body. During pain or ailments, this will prove to be an elixir for you. Not only will it ease your pain, but shall also put you on the path of regaining good health. Likewise, follow this practice with your ideologies and beliefs as well. For, as far as beliefs and ideologies are concerned, every person here has created their own 'me', 'mine' and 'my own'. In essence, you need to weaken all your delusions of 'me', 'mine' and 'my own'. For, it is only this delusion that increases the distance between you and your Soul. Hence, whenever you are gripped by a negativity due to the delusion of 'me', 'mine' and 'my own', practise the above-mentioned exercise to get rid of it. With this one experiment, you shall continue to inch closer to the Soul.

Practise deep breathing every morning and night

At the outset, first let us understand; where is the Soul located in the body? Well, it rests in the navel. In other words, you experience the presence of the Soul in the depths of your navel. But how can one reach there? It is indeed not so easy! For, you have surrounded yourself with several blockages of 'me', 'mine' and 'my own'. Even so, a simple regimen will do the trick. Upon waking up in the morning and before sleeping at night, sit in solitude with a calm mind, and for five minutes, just take deep breaths. Ensure that each breath you take is long and deep, and reaches your navel. With this, the blockages of 'me', 'mine' and 'my own' that have been created between you and your Soul shall weaken gradually. These deep breaths will break the barriers and weaken all your blockages of 'me', 'mine' and 'my own' and reach the Soul. With this exercise, your experience of self-realisation will automatically strengthen by the day.

Who am I?

Every morning upon waking up, close your eyes for ten minutes, sit in contemplation and ask yourself, "Who am I? Am I this house? Am I the car I drive or the degree I hold? Am I the money or the relationships? Am I the body? Am I the brain and ego?" And while contemplating over this, experience the feeling of detachment grow with reference to these possessions and belongings. And then reply to your own question, "No, not at all. I am neither wealth nor academic qualifications; nor am I the body or the brain-ego. I am just the Soul and the powerful minds."

By repeating these affirmations regularly with concentration in a state of relaxation, you shall begin to inch closer to your '*shunya*'–nothingness i.e. your Soul.

Anything you do–do it with profundity

You are the Soul, and the Soul is the most profound power and the deepest layer of a human being. Thus, what actions you indulge in on the outside or what you experience within is not the moot question. The important question is, whether the task has been accomplished through the strength of your Soul or your brain-ego. The question is not of what you are experiencing, rather the question is whether that experience is profound or just at the peripheral level? If you experience it superficially, you are most certainly distanced from your Soul. But if the feeling is intense and profound, you are definitely close to the Soul.

In short, action per se doesn't matter. It doesn't matter what you are doing or what act you are indulging in, whether it is cooking, reading a book, working in office or playing. What matters is, whether you are performing that task superficially or are deeply involved in it? If you are deeply involved in the task, you will not only be focussed on it, but will also enjoy it wholeheartedly. If this is not the case, then know it with certainty that you are doing it superficially, just at the peripheral level. And it is but certain that constant engagement in tasks at the peripheral level will continue to drift you away from the Soul. Thus, anytime, anything you do, do it deeply and intensely. This constant habit of carrying out tasks with deep involvement will take you closer to your Soul, before you even realise it. 'You' will change; your centre of existence with which you have identified will shift from the brain-ego and weaker minds to the powerful minds and Soul.

In the same vein, it doesn't matter whether you are happy or sad. What matters is whether that emotion is experienced at a superficial level or in depth. Then it doesn't matter if you are so depressed that you are tagged as a lamenter or a 'downer'. But if your emotion is so deep and intense, then it is the sorrow of the Soul. In short, whether it is your deeds or your emotions, they all should be intense and deep in nature, as close to the Soul as possible. Only then you shall remain in close proximity to the Soul. Therefore, I hope, you shall henceforth refrain from performing tasks at a superficial level, whether it is an act of appreciation or gratefulness...you will only do it wholeheartedly. Being superficially good may please others, but that will not serve you any purpose. Everyone indulges in such superficial acts, but what do they gain eventually? You will stand to gain only when it is done wholeheartedly, from deep within. I hope, you must have grasped this plain and simple fact, and hereon, you shall begin to live from your depths, thereby increasing your proximity to your Soul.

Every week, weaken one attachment of 'Me', 'Mine' and 'My Own'

Here, a pertinent point to ponder upon is, what is the distance between you and your Soul? The distance comprises everything that you have accumulated on the strength of brain-ego under the delusion of 'me', 'mine' and 'my own'. Then it doesn't matter whether they are objects, human beings, thoughts or beliefs. For the inner power, they are all termites that gnaw from inside and create hollowness within. Thus, you need to do two things; firstly, refrain from creating new attachments of 'me', 'mine' and 'my own', and simultaneously, every week, detach from one bondage of 'me', 'mine' and 'my own'. Have faith that with every detachment, you will automatically continue to grow closer to the Soul. Always remember, that deluded by the notions of 'me', 'mine' and 'my own', this treasure that you have presumed as 'your own', is actually not 'yours'. On the contrary, it is the very root of your sorrows and failures. Hence, the sooner you disconnect from them, the better your life will be.

Just think, whether it is your car or your house, your wife or your son, if you don't assume them as yours and detach yourself from them, will they become someone else's? No! They will still belong to you! Only the connection will break; that is, you will continue to enjoy their presence, but will be free of the troubles and stress ensued by any vicissitudes in them. And the more you become free of those pains and stresses, the closer you shall be inching towards your Soul. As a result, even when friends and objects change on the outside, you will not endure stress as they will not belong to you anymore. You will surely experience the joy they bring, but they will be mere fellow travellers for you. They will only be 'mediums' for you, who would be instrumental for specific things in life and who are meant to meet and part ways. In other words, you shall transform and become like Krishna. In the external world, you shall have the entire golden city of Dwarka, with everyone looking up to you as *Dwarkadheesh* – The King of Dwarka, but deep inside, none of it will belong to you. You will certainly take pleasure in all of it, but will not harbour the pain that comes with any ups and downs in it. And this is the zenith of human life; be a conqueror on the outside but dwell in absolute nothingness within.

Having explained the concept of Soul in detail, I shall now end this discussion in the hope, that even you shall now have your own golden city of Dwarka in the external world and dwell in nothingness within. You will continue to dwell in your Dwarka, admire it, revel in it, but you shall always maintain the awareness that 'Dwarka' does not belong to you. Similarly, the body is not yours either. And at the height of meditative awareness, you shall well comprehend your body to be separate from you. Hence, set forth on the journey to inch closer to your Soul, experience and revel in its powers, and in the process, be a witness and enjoy the spectacle of how your life catapults to unprecedented heights of freedom, joy and wonder.

Bestseller by **Deep Trivedi**

'I am The Mind' by Deep Trivedi is carving a readership of its own. In this book, the author has revealed secrets of the mind and has provided answers to questions related to every aspect of life such as family, business, career, etc. Till now, hundreds and thousands of people have not just read the book, but have also imbibed the instructions in their daily life and experienced an instantaneous transformation.

The book provides answers to mind-boggling questions such as:

- How did a barely educated Edison become a scientist with more than a thousand patents registered in his name?
- How did Dhirubhai Ambani, who at one time was a petrol station attendant, become such a big industrialist?
- How did a barely educated, naughty boy become Steve Jobs?

NATIONAL BESTSELLER

OVER 1,00,000 COPIES SOLD

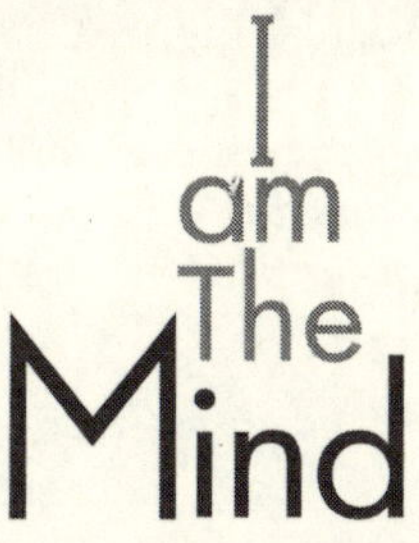

The Master Key

to achieve anything you want!

Available in English, Hindi, Marathi, Gujarati, Malayalam & Tamil
at **www.aatmanestore.com**, all other leading book stores & e-commerce sites

Other Bestsellers by **Deep Trivedi**

'101 All Time Great Stories With Life-changing Philosophies' is a book of fascinating short stories that will transport you into the world of great men, artists and philosophers. In this book, author Deep Trivedi has penned many famous stories and anecdotes, in his simple, humorous and inimitable style, which aims to create psychological awareness in life.

Thought-provoking stories that are not just interesting to read, but that will also bring about a positive change in your life.

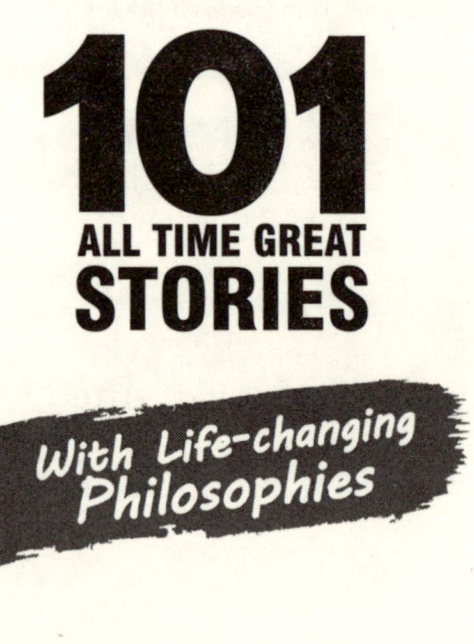

Available in English, Hindi, Marathi and Gujarati at **aatmanestore.com** and all other leading book stores and e-commerce sites

Other Bestsellers by **Deep Trivedi**

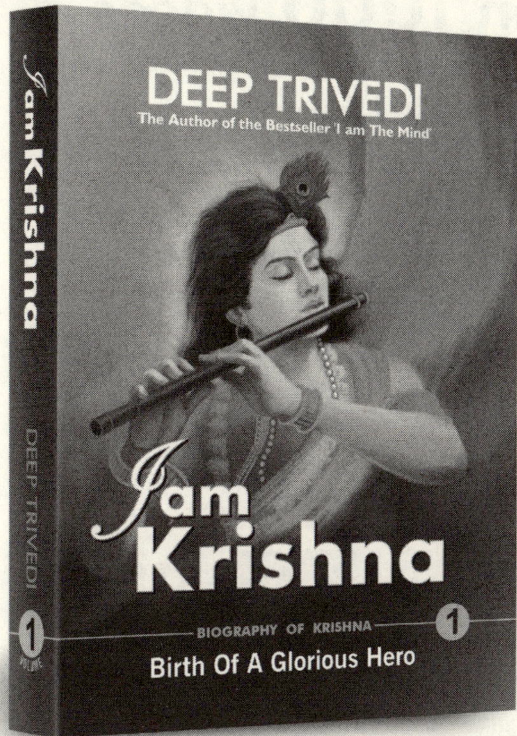

I am Krishna

- An Artist
- A Lover
- A Spiritual Guru
- A Politician
- A Businessman
- A Visionary
- A Psychologist

NOW AVAILABLE

Available in English, Hindi and Gujarati at **www.aatmanestore.com**
and all other leading book stores and e-commerce sites

Follow Deep Trivedi's Magic on YouTube

More than 1000 videos

on different subjects related to Human Life, Human Psychology and Laws of Nature

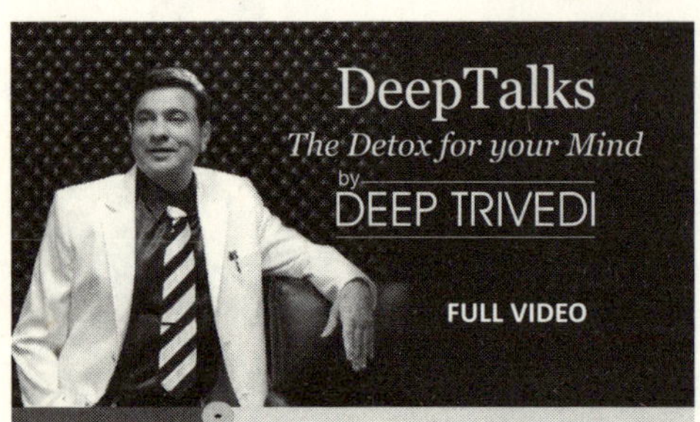

Watch full lectures on different topics by Deep Trivedi and DeepAnswers on his YouTube channel - **www.youtube.com/deeptrivedivideos** where he resolves queries of his followers as a friend, philosopher and guide.

संपूर्ण भगवद्गीता (हिन्दी में) अध्याय 1–18

कबीर के अद्भुत 200+ दोहे

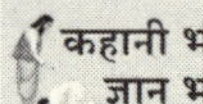

कहानी भी ज्ञान भी

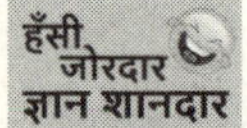

हँसी जोरदार ज्ञान शानदार

महानतम गुरु कृष्ण से सीखें

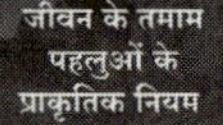

जीवन के तमाम पहलुओं के प्राकृतिक नियम

DeepTalks TAO TE CHING by DEEP TRIVEDI

DeepTalks bhagavad gita by DEEP TRIVEDI

DeepTalks Ashtavakra Gita by DEEP TRIVEDI

DeepTalks Secrets by DEEP TRIVEDI

WORKSHOPS by DEEP TRIVEDI

To avail other titles or DeepTalks DVDs and Audio CDs, visit **aatmanestore.com** and all leading e-commerce sites.

Scan it

You can also follow him on Facebook, Instagram and Twitter

  **@deeptrivediblog**